Household of Freedom

Published by The Westminster Press

Books by Letty M. Russell

Household of Freedom: Authority in Feminist Theology

Becoming Human *(Library of Living Faith)*

Growth in Partnership

The Future of Partnership

Human Liberation in a Feminist Perspective—A Theology

Christian Education in Mission

Books edited by Letty M. Russell

Feminist Interpretation of the Bible

The Liberating Word:
A Guide to Nonsexist Interpretation of the Bible

Household of Freedom
Authority in Feminist Theology
The 1986 Annie Kinkead Warfield Lectures

Letty M. Russell

The Westminster Press
Philadelphia

Scripture quotations from the Revised Standard Version of the Bible are copyrighted 1946, 1952, ©1971, 1973 by the Division of Christian Education of the National Council of the Churches of Christ in the U.S.A. and are used by permission.

Book design by Gene Harris

First edition

Published by The Westminster Press®
Philadelphia, Pennsylvania

PRINTED IN THE UNITED STATES OF AMERICA

9 8 7 6 5 4 3

Acknowledgments

Grateful acknowledgment is made to the following publishers for permission to use previously published material:

Christian Kaiser Verlag: Letty M. Russell, "Theology of the Future in Feminist Theology," in *Gottes Zukunft—Zukunft der Welt*, ed. by J. Deuser, G. M. Martin, K. Stock, M. Welker (Munich, 1986).

Princeton Theological Seminary: Letty M. Russell, "People and the Powers," *Princeton Seminary Bulletin*, vol. 8, no. 1 (February 1987).

The Religious Education Association: Letty M. Russell, "Inclusive Language and Power," *Religious Education*, vol. 80, no. 4 (Fall 1985), pp. 582–602.

The Trinity Institute: Letty M. Russell, "Authority and Hope in Feminist Theology," 1987.

The United Methodist Publishing House and the United Methodist Board of Higher Education and Ministry: for permission to reprint in modified form, in chapter 6, material from Letty M. Russell, "Authority in Mutual Ministry," *Quarterly Review: A Scholarly Journal for Reflection on Ministry*, Spring 1986, ©copyright 1986.

Library of Congress Cataloging-in-Publication Data

Russell, Letty M.
  Household of freedom.

  (The 1986 Annie Kinkead Warfield lectures)
  Bibliography: p.
  1. Authority (Religion) 2. Woman (Christian
theology) I. Title. II. Series: Annie Kinkead
Warfield lectures; 1986.
BT88.R87 1987   262'.8   86–18992
ISBN 0-664-24017-8

Shannon

Contents

Preface
and Acknowledgments

It was a great honor to deliver an earlier version of these six chapters as the Annie Kinkead Warfield Lectures at Princeton Theological Seminary in 1986. It is fortunate that the lectures were named for Benjamin Warfield's wife, for I am sure he would not have been very excited about discussions of "Authority in Feminist Theology"! According to a recent issue of *The Journal of Presbyterian History*, this Princeton patriarch was "the country's most scholarly—and most unyielding—opponent of the so-called liberal theology."[1] His vigorous defense of the plenary verbal inspiration of scriptures was instrumental in winning the day for what was known as "Princeton theology."

The topic of authority, however, is very important in Reformed theological tradition and thus fulfills Warfield's request. Doctrines of authority were much on the minds of the Reformers. According to Margaret Miles, authority was the greatest problem they faced because they eliminated the visual images of hierarchy in the churches and preached of spiritual equality.[2] Small wonder that some of the "murdering and robbing peasants" and outspoken women got out of hand!

Authority is a crucial theological problem for us today as well. We also live in a time of great ferment and change, when many persons begin to assert the possibility of structural equality in their lives. In this period of late-industrial capitalism the world finds itself in the midst of radical social crisis, and we try to understand that world in terms of history, pluralism, and change.[3] In the midst of this change, white male Western culture moves farther and farther away from the sources of Hebrew and Hellenistic culture that gave it birth. Even the word "authority" no longer has its original Latin meaning of going back to the founding fathers, the authors of Roman society. In Hannah Arendt's opinion we do not even have authority any more, because we are no longer connected with our sources of life.[4] As Christians we find ourselves trying to explain why it is that the biblical faith still makes sense in our lives, and often we end up trying to protect the living Word by reducing it to a rigid and unchanging pattern of doctrine.

In *Word and Faith*, Gerhard Ebeling has given us a classic description of the challenge of historicity. "For modern [persons] everything, the whole of reality, turns to history. . . . Whatever the problem that is taken up, it transforms itself . . . into a historical problem."[5] Ebeling compares this problem to the touch of King Midas, the legendary Phrygian king to whom Dionysus granted the power of turning everything he touched into gold. The same could be said for the problem of authority, especially in regard to feminist theology. For whatever feminist theologians take up transforms itself into an authority problem. I usually call this the "feminist touch"—referring not to holding hands but to the daily experience of women who find that their words, actions, and being tend to raise questions of authority within a society and church that assumes authority only comes in the male gender.

For example, I entered Harvard Divinity School in 1954, the first year women were admitted to study for the ministry. When I graduated, the faculty was reluctant to grant top honors to the only two women in the class because it might reflect poorly on the qualifications of the men. In 1962 I attended a World Council of Churches meeting in Switzerland. There a Russian bishop expended no little effort to tell me, through an interpreter, what he thought of uppity women pastors from East Harlem, N.Y. He told a parable of a monk who was very proud of his ability to walk on water—until he drowned! At Princeton in 1974, I taught a pastor in the summer session who was sure that everything I said about the meaning of vocation was radical and heretical because I was a woman. When I finally convinced him that what I was saying was very much in line with such authority figures as Calvin and Barth, he decided that it was not worthwhile to attend my lectures because I didn't know anything new!

These minor incidents are similar to countless others told by women around the world. As with so many other women in ministry, my very being has been considered a threat to established authority. Whatever women do in a role that claims academic or ecclesiastical authority tends to be interpreted as a threat if authority is seen as a masculine attribute. In such a predicament, it is no wonder that I consider the problem of authority to be a crucial feminist issue. I am happy to join the Reformers in trying to make sense of the Christian faith in a world of change. And I would not be surprised if we all found it helpful to explore how authority is imaged in our lives and in our communities of faith.

In the following chapters I will be discussing authority in feminist theology, trying to analyze the problems of authority in an eschatological perspective and to present some alternative ways of imaging how authority might function in a household of freedom.

Chapter 1 introduces the theme "Authority of the Future," looking at the importance of an appeal to God's promised future of a household of freedom, for both Christians and feminists, and then turning to perspectives on authority and power.

The second chapter, "Paradigms of Authority," explores the possibility of shifting from paradigms of domination to those of partnership. This shift is seen in the work of feminist and liberation theologies as well as in the writings of all theologians concerned for the survival of this earth.

Chapter 3, "Power of Naming," analyzes the authority of God's Word and the power of God-talk. By way of example, it explores the possibility of thinking of God as Housekeeper of all creation.

The fourth chapter, "New House of Authority," asks how the old house was built up through biblical and church tradition and proposes that we begin to interpret authority from the perspective of those at the bottom of society. Perhaps a new perspective will lead us out of the "master's house" toward a place to call our home.

Chapter 5, "Household, Power, and Glory," continues the housekeeping theme. Analyzing the way Christ's power was sustained in weakness leads to an understanding of messianic politics, and the future vision of the household of God empowers people to contend against the principalities and powers of this present age.

The final chapter, "Good Housekeeping," is concerned with the mending of the church. The way authority can be shared in community is highlighted through discussion of problems of paternalism and autonomy and of strategies for working out partnership in households of freedom.

In this book I am constantly aware of the style of authority exercised in the life and teachings of Jesus of Nazareth. Over and over in the New Testament we are exhorted to take on this style of authority in the form of servanthood. As Paul says:

> Have this mind among yourselves, which is yours in Christ Jesus, who, though being in the form of God, did not count equality with God a thing to be grasped, but emptied self, taking the form of a servant, being born in the likeness of human beings (Phil. 2:5–7).[6]

The reason for sharing together in theological reflections on authority is to take these teachings seriously, to analyze the way that authority functions as domination and not as empowerment for service. It is my contention that feminist theology in its constant struggle with the feminist touch will at least provide us with an occasion for analyzing the way we live out the gospel mandate. This book is an invitation to explore ways of including all the people of God in the sharing of authority in a household of freedom.

The book is dedicated to the many persons who have participated in its preparation, and especially to Shannon Clarkson. The interest and response of so many persons and groups to the discussion of authority have greatly encouraged me in my writing. The first draft was developed from lectures in response to the invitation of a number of institutions, including Garrett-Evangelical Theological Seminary, The Shalom Center and Luther Northwestern Theological Seminary, Moravian Theological Seminary, Princeton Theological Seminary, The Trinity Institute, and United Theological Seminary. I would like to extend my special thanks to Katharine Doob Sakenfeld, Margaret Farley, and to my editor, Cynthia Thompson, as well as to Yale Divinity School and to the students who shared with me in so many class sessions on authority.

Household of Freedom

1

Authority
of the Future

I have spoken on many panels about women and ministry since my ordination as a Presbyterian minister in 1958. But one such panel at Union Theological Seminary in 1969 stands out in my memory. I do not remember what I said, but I probably shared some of my experiences as a pastor in East Harlem and discussed biblical arguments for and against women's ordination. What I remember very well was the main lecture delivered by Peggy Ann Way on "An Authority of Possibility for Women in the Church." She claimed that the authority of her ministry was rooted in her own religious experience as it "intersected with Scripture, history, myth, the church, cultural analysis, and people experiences."[1] Like many other feminist theologians, Peggy Way appealed to her own experience as a woman as a test of traditional church authority in the face of the sexist practices of the churches. Yet at the same time she was expressing her faith in a God who holds open the future possibility of new creation.

Since that time a great deal of feminist theory and practice has served to clarify the meaning of feminism and the possibilities of feminist theology. Yet the question of authority is still a source of interest and debate, and the experience of women is still a norm for the truthfulness of tradition. Like other liberation theologies, feminist theologies recognize the importance of experience and context in the formation of all theologies as well as in the formation of scripture, tradition, and paradigms of rationality. But the very fact that *women's* experience is appealed to as an authority in theology is often cause for disbelief on the part of white male theological establishments.[2] And this disbelief is compounded when the experience claimed is not just female (biological) or feminine (cultural). It is the feminist (political) experience of those advocating a change of society to include both women and men as human beings, created in God's image to participate with God in the fashioning of new creation.

There is no one description of feminist or one type of feminist theology, but there is a consensus that a feminist is one who advocates the human dignity and equality of women and men. Such advocacy includes all women and men, not just those who are white educated inhabitants of North Atlantic nations. Although I write as a white middle-class Protestant from the northeastern United States, and speak out of that context, as a feminist I am committed to working for the equality of all women and men of every race, class, and nationality. This commitment of those who call themselves feminist is underlined by Barbara Smith, in an article on "Racism and Women's Studies," by the way she defines feminism.

> Feminism is the political theory and practice that struggles to free *all* women: women of color, working-class women, poor women, disabled women, lesbians, old women—as well as white, economically privileged, heterosexual women. Anything less than this vision of total freedom is not feminism, but merely female self-aggrandizement.[3]

Feminist theologies seek to act and reflect upon this search for liberation from all forms of dehumanization, joining God in advocating full human dignity of each and every person.

Appeal to the Future

In this process of advocacy, appeal to the authority of the future becomes an important aspect of feminist theology. Women can appeal to the authority of their experience, but this experience is primarily of the old creation and of the structures of patriarchy in church and society. We do not yet know what real live children of God will look like (Rom. 8:19). Therefore, we take the *via negativa* and describe the contradictions of our past and present social, political, economic, and ecclesial experiences. But at the same time, we live out of a vision of God's intention for a mended creation, and it is this hope that helps us "keep on keeping on."[4] In an important sense Christian feminists only have this future, for the patriarchal structures of scripture, tradition, church, and theology are such that the process of reconstruction of women's place in man's world requires a utopian faith that understand's God's future as an impulse for change in the present. As Beverly Harrison points out, the work of feminist theology is not only to identify and analyze the past and present order of things, but also to engage in "utopic envisagement."[5]

Distortion of the past. Even the reconstruction of the lives of our foremothers in the scriptures and church tradition is not without discouragement. What is do:umented in the forgotten lives of women is the difficulty of their lives and the ways in which their characters and names have been dishonored or erased. For instance, in speaking of Mary Magdalene, the woman who was healed by Jesus and became his disciple (Luke 8:2), Elisabeth Moltmann-Wendel has written that patriarchal distortion of history transformed her story.

> Mary Magdalene had been made into the exemplary monster and model of sin and sexuality because her dazzling, privileged, and unique story offered the possibility of releasing imaginative fantasies.[6]

The woman who had been known as "the Apostle to the Apostles" became falsely identified with the woman sinner of Luke 7:37 and with the anointing of Mary of Bethany (John 12:3).

Her foremother Miriam fared no better in the tradition of the Hebrew scriptures. Although she was probably an independent leader in Israel, Miriam was made a sister of Aaron and Moses in the later tradition (Num. 26:59). According to Exodus 15:20 she was a prophet who proclaimed God's triumph over Pharaoh.[7] Numbers 12 describes what happens to Miriam when she usurps authority. With Aaron she challenges the sole authority of Moses by saying, "Has the Lord indeed spoken only through Moses?" The patriarchal tradition then proceeds to diminish Miriam, punish her with leprosy, and drop her from the story, until mentioning that she was buried in Kadesh (Num. 20:1). Phyllis Trible has pointed out, however, that Miriam is not forgotten by the people. They refuse to march for fifteen days, until Miriam has been brought back into the camp (Num. 12:15), and her memory lives on in the prophetic tradition until a new Miriam, Mary, becames the Mother of the Deliverer.[8] The claim of women to speak with the authority of God continues to be "dangerous to their health," but women continue to reconstruct the past of their foremothers in order to gain strength to speak with authority of the future that God intends for all people. As Rosemary Ruether has put it:

> One does not have to lose or repudiate one's past to claim the right to build a new future, in which the divine is experienced from women's perspective in a way not previously allowed or, at least, not remembered by a religious tradition biased by patriarchy.[9]

Revolution of freedom. Feminist theology is part of a revolution of consciousness that touches the issue of authority at every turn. In appealing to a paradigm of authority in community, it challenges both the content and the thought structure of Christian theology as we know it. As women challenge patriarchal authority, they may expect a fate similar to that of Miriam unless they can join with those women and men who are willing to appeal from the present, not simply to past tradition but also to the memory of the future. For it is this authority of God's new creation that holds open the promise of Galatians 3:28 that there is neither Jew nor Greek, slave nor free, male nor female, but that all are one in Christ Jesus.

In this sense, then, feminist Christians appeal to the future as the source of authority. They appeal to God's future action in creating the world as a household where both humanity and nature can live in a community of responsibility and freedom, and they claim that this future action is already present in the action of God through the people of Israel and through Jesus Christ. Biblical theology itself is "hope filled" and provides images of jubilee and liberation, images of promise on the way to fulfillment. Thus our memory of the future becomes an appeal to the future of the oppressed, the marginal, the "little ones" of God's *oikos* (household), for whom the scriptures hold out a vision of new society. Standing in solidarity with those who "hope against hope," feminist theologians seek to articulate the vision of a mended creation in the midst of the structures of domination that perpetuate suffering in our tattered and torn creation. Such an appeal to the future is not a flight from present reality but a commitment to contribute to the actualization of hope.[10]

In his 1968 essay "The Revolution of Freedom," Jürgen Moltmann pointed out that there has been a succession of freedom movements that have expressed the human striving for liberation in Western society. Each new movement has continued the gains of previous ones and attempted to overcome the continuing disappointments, but "so far, no one of them has brought about the 'realm of freedom' itself, but each one has opened a new front in the struggle for freedom."[11] From time to time, women have opened up a new front in their own struggle for liberation, only to find that the patriarchal structures of authority overwhelm their contribution. This time women join with oppressed peoples from many different societies as they participate in their own movements toward liberation, making the claim that women and their concerns must be partners in every struggle for freedom if the future is to be open for all people.

My contention in this book is that authority is a key issue in this part of the revolution of freedom. In order to see this more clearly, it is necessary to provide a working description of authority and power as they open up the possibility of living in new households of freedom.

Perspectives on Authority

People often confuse the meanings of power and authority. Living each day with the experience of their dynamics, they notice that both seem to result in various forms of dominance or coercion. And there is good reason for this commonsense understanding. Although sociologists disagree in their theories of social stratification, they probably agree in the analysis of power and authority as dominance. Functionalists, describing the social interactions and needs of society, frequently report that authority happens as domination and that power gravitates "to the top." Conflict theorists, focusing on competition for scarce resources, continually highlight ways that social, political, and economic inequality lead to patterns of elitism and oppression.[12] But there is a great deal more to be said about these patterns of human relationships and how they might be understood from a Christian and a feminist perspective.

Legitimated power. In order to establish a working description of this dynamic process at work in our lives and societies, I will venture a schematic description here that can be amplified and tested as we move through the following chapters. My intention is to understand *power as the ability to accomplish desired ends* and social power as the ability of one individual or group to affect the behavior of another individual or group.[13] The focus of power is on the subject who initiates the change, with or without consent of the respondent. Power is exercised through influence or force and is usually competitive. In situations of power exchange we tend to ask the question, "Should I do it?" We weigh the consequences of noncompliance against those of compliance in deciding how to respond.

I understand *authority as legitimated power.*[14] It accomplishes its ends by evoking the assent of the respondent. Authority is more than a form of power; it is power that is legitimated by the structures of society. It is exercised in most situations through hierarchy and is control.[15] In relationships of authority we tend to ask the question "Why should I?" The subject's right to make the request is assumed by the respondent, who nevertheless questions the reasons for the request.[16] Thus in growing up as children we accept our parents' right to tell us to go to bed, but we always ask

"Why? Why?" As grown-ups we continue to assume that sources of authority have a right to that form of influence, but we engage in discussions of how that right functions. An obvious example of this in our own settings is the amount of attention given to *why* and *how* the Bible has authority by those who have experienced that indeed it does evoke their assent and guide their lives.

All human relationships include the dynamics of authority and power. From a psychosocial point of view the relational bonds of authority provide needed images of strength in our lives.[17] The problem is that the relationships are often distorted and manipulated, and authority then takes on the form of domination or even tyranny. When this happens, authority is eroded and becomes illegitimate power. For example, in the Watergate hearings, the authority of the U.S. Presidency was questioned because of its misuse by Richard Nixon and his associates, and he was denied the right to the structural authority of the presidential office. Human beings cannot function without structures of authority, but they can seek out structures that contribute to communal well-being and justice.

There are many different ways that the relational bond of authority is established. Besides the *structural authority* that comes from a position of influence in the social, economic, and political spheres of the world, there is *authority of knowledge*, which is considered valuable by those who give assent. *Charismatic authority* is usually gained because particular persons have the ability to gain the assent of others through their gifts as leaders and speakers. *Authority of wisdom* comes to those who through long experience develop an understanding of the world and human nature that helps others to cope with their lives.

All these bonds of relationship, and others as well, interact with each other so that respondents assent to what they consider the legitimated power of a person, text, or governmental structure. For instance, as a teacher and lecturer I exercise forms of legitimated power or authority. Those who listen to a lecture are usually assenting to the fact that I have a right to give the lecture, even though they keep asking "Why? Why?" and arguing with what I say. This authority rests initially on my structural position as a professor at Yale, which legitimates my right to lecture. Over the course of a lecture, however, assent would be eroded unless what was said appeared to make sense and was rooted in the authority of knowledge. In the course of time I might also discover authority of wisdom or charismatic authority in relation to certain groups of persons. Together, these and other factors establish the relationship of assent, which can provide a rich resource

for dialogue and mutual learning but also may be misused to in-
doctrinate persons with my point of view. In either case, the way
I or anyone else exercises authority and power determines
whether it is authority as domination or as partnership.

Power and authority are usually associated with domination,
competition, and control. But do they need to be understood this
way? From the perspective of the Christian gospel and from the
perspective of feminist theory the answer is *no*. Power and authority can be exercised through domination and they most frequently
are, in a world patterned by patriarchal paradigms of reality. But
they can also be exercised through empowerment and authorizing, as they sometimes are where people are seeking to live out the
gospel vision of shared community of service. This form of relationship has some very clear precedent in biblical theology, both
as a lived reality and as a hoped-for promise of a new house of
freedom (Gal. 5:1).

Source of authority. The self-revelation of God in Jesus Christ
and through the Spirit is the source of authority in our lives as
Christians. Thus the foundation of our lives is the faith claim that
there is a God who is the source of life and love and that this God
has chosen to be with us as Emmanuel. As Karl Barth has re-
minded us, God wants to be our partner and savior and has shown
this in choosing to share our humanity.[18] In the New Testament
we hear of a God whose authority works through the power of
love. In hearing the story of that love in the life, death, and resurrection of Jesus Christ, we "fall in faith." It is only in the later
theological development that we come to hear of a God who rules
as "an omnipotent, impassable, immutable, Caesar-god," rather
than a God of suffering love and servant ministry.[19] As Jürgen
Moltmann said in his speech with Elisabeth Moltmann-Wendel at
the World Council of Churches' Sheffield Consultation on the
Community of Women and Men in the Church, this accommodation of Christianity to patriarchy

> had a crippling effect on its liberating potential, as has been per-
> ceived by theologians of hope, liberation theologians, and political
> theologians in other contexts, when they criticized the "Constantin-
> ian captivity" of the church. It has now been fully demonstrated by
> feminist theology.[20]

Christian community has a pattern of criteria for what is an
authoritative witness to God in Jesus Christ. Usually that configu-
ration includes the resources of scientific knowledge and human
experience as well as those of scripture and church tradition. David Kelsey has pointed out that there are limits on theological

interpretation as it seeks to discern this pattern of meaning. These limits are rooted in the need to continue to witness to the gospel message and thus they must be in touch with the biblical and church tradition, as well as being intelligible and seriously imaginable in a particular cultural setting.[21]

Whatever the pattern of criteria may be for a particular church, it is not the pattern itself that has authority. It is the connection of that pattern with the divine self-revelation of God that gives it authority and limits its claims. For Christians, an important criterion is consistency with the exercise of authority in Jesus' ministry. When we look at the Gospels we discover that Jesus has authority as the agent inaugurating the kingdom of God (God's new creation). Although the kingship metaphors are drawn from the contemporary social patterns of understanding, the content of this kingship is quite different. It was so different, in fact, that the disciples never seemed to have understood it and were always waiting for Jesus to expel the Romans and claim his throne. Madeleine Boucher reminds us that Jesus "rejected every authority role of his patriarchal tradition which the Messiah had been expected to assume."[22] His authority (*exousia*) and power (*dynamis*) were gifts of God for the work of ushering in the New Age. Jesus had authority to forgive sins, cast out unclean spirits, and preach the good news. He taught with authority because he spoke of God's will directly and not only on the basis of scriptural interpretation (Mark 1:22).

The Gospels describe power in Jesus' ministry as the power to heal. There is no indication that he used his power to dominate. Rather, he was one who proclaimed release to the captives and brought sight to the blind. He proclaimed God's radical reversal of the status quo, as the very ones who were the least in society were empowered for new life in God's kingdom (Luke 4:18–19). The authority of Jesus' ministry is also to become the authority of his disciples and followers. They are to forgive, to cast out evil, to heal and preach good news. The authority of this ministry of service and care is the life-style of Jesus Christ. The mutual ministry of the church only shares this authority when its witness in word is lived out in actions of love so that the Word of God continues to be incarnated in our world. In this sense the authority of faith which builds on this foundation is every bit as much dependent on its *orthopraxy* as upon its *orthodoxy*. A teaching evokes our consent when we see it leading toward the actualization of Christ's ministry in both word and deed.

When we look at the root meaning of the English word "authority," we discover that the Latin word *auctoritas* derives from the verb *augere*, meaning to augment or increase. As Hannah Arendt reminds us, our concept of authority in Western civilization derives from the Roman idea that those in authority constantly augment the foundation of the ancestors or founders of Rome.[23] In this perspective, authority—as the right to influence because of relationship to the origins of life, faith, and society—forms the Roman patriarchal paradigm. The authority of the founding fathers is understood as the legitimization or authorizing of domination in politics, culture, and household. Although Greek culture had no equivalent concept for authority in politics, the Greeks had a clear image of its use and usefulness, not in the democratic *polis* but in the monarchical *oikos*, or household. According to Aristotle it was the natural order of things that the household be set up in a hierarchy with the master ruling over the wife, children, and slaves.[24]

This does sound a little familiar even if we haven't read any Greek philosophy lately. Not only are the "household tables" or instructions in the Pastoral Epistles greatly influenced by this Greek and Roman understanding, but we also are influenced by it. We often picture authority of the scriptures in terms of the founding events of our faith, and we continue to believe that an orderly household needs to have someone in charge. In order to break out of this idea of authority rooted in a timeless patriarchal *archetype*, some feminist theologians such as Elisabeth Fiorenza have turned to the idea of *prototype*, as a model of the past that is not binding or unchanging but rather "is critically open to the possibility of its own transformation."[25] Others, such as myself, have turned to the idea of authority rooted not just in the past but in the anticipation of God's intended future. In either case the intention of feminist theologians is to keep open to the possibility that God is doing a new thing, and this new thing may have to do with the way we exercise authority in God's world household (Jer. 31:22).[26]

Household of Freedom

Ordinarily in our privatistic culture the image evoked by the word "household" is that of a small family cut off from the public sector and often beset with interpersonal problems. Yet there is no one form of house or household either in the biblical accounts or in the many cultures that dwell on earth. In order to be able to celebrate this diversity of concrete households gathered in so many different ways around the world, it is important to remember that all households are linked together in God's *oikos*, or world house. The false dualism of the city-state, *polis* (the arena of free men with property), and the household, *oikos* (the arena of wives, slaves, and children ruled over by "free" men), that is found in ancient Greek society condemns the *oikos* to be a household of bondage, a miniature replica of what was to become the larger household of Caesar that spread across the Roman empire. It also leaves the *polis* to be a false democracy, based on oppression of the families and the work force of the society.

In opposition to this dualism and its resulting oppression, I want to argue that it is possible to begin with the biblical understanding of God's *oikonomia*, or householding of the whole earth, and thus be able to describe the exercise of authority in both the private and the public realms as a participation in God's householding and partnering activity. As we will see in chapter 2, "household of freedom" as a metaphor describes the concrete human interaction that takes place in our interdependent societies, but it breaks open the oppressive experiences of household by speaking of it as a household where freedom dwells. This experience of household is both a future and present reality. Just as the New Testament speaks of the kingdom or household of God in terms of "already, not yet," it is possible to speak of household of freedom as a present experience of women and men who glimpse the intention of God's household as they share authority in community with one another.

"Household of freedom" is a metaphor for the glimpses of God's household that we catch from time to time in our own relationships. In chapter 5 I will also want to argue that "household of God" can be used as an alternative translation of the phrase "kingdom of God." In this sense household of God does not refer to the church, as it does in later New Testament books such as 1 Peter, but rather to God's new creation. Insofar as church in all its manifestations becomes a place where household of freedom is experienced, it also becomes a sign of God's household.

A house divided. Households of freedom are few and far between, yet they are experienced from time to time as people struggle against forms of bondage and discover glimpses of a new reality for their lives. One such story of a divided house that becomes a house of freedom is found in Margaret Walker's 1966 novel *Jubilee*, about the daily life of "slavocracy" during the Civil War.[27] Walker shows the results of division and domination in the plantation and in the national household.

> If a kingdom is divided against itself, that kingdom cannot stand. And if a house is divided against itself, that house will not be able to stand (Mark 3:24–25).

The manor in *Jubilee* is a house divided. In the "Big House" dwells Dutton with his wife and two children. In the slave quarters dwell Vyry—Elvira—and the other fourteen children fathered by Dutton and born through the pain, suffering, and death of the slave woman Hetta. Amid the jubilees or songs of her people, Elvira Ware Brown manages to join her husband, Innis Brown, in building a house of freedom where there is a possibility of wholeness and partnership even in the face of continuing danger and racism.[28]

This picture of the divided house is very different from *Gone with the Wind*, written thirty years earlier by Margaret Mitchell.[29] This, rather than the alternative history of a black woman's struggle toward new forms of shared authority, has held the imagination of the U.S. public. It is the saga of Atlanta in all its powerful nostalgia for the old "slavocracy" that causes it to continue as a best-seller, even after fifty years. Unfortunately, much of the racism of our nation is not "gone with the wind"; and it continues in a house divided where freedom is granted only to those whose skin, class, and sex allow them to participate fully in the *polis*. Yet the powerful biblical images of liberation continue to catch our imagination and call us to seek out alternatives to the divisions of our world.

Memory of the future. One of these is the image of jubilee that evokes a powerful memory of the future in Jewish and Christian history. In Hebrew tradition, jubilee is God's protest against oppression of the people and of the land, as it recalls the Sabbath tradition of rest for all the creation as well as the deliverance from slavery. In her book *Jesus, Liberation, and the Biblical Jubilee*, Sharon Ringe traces the image of jubilee through biblical tradition. What seems to have been a social proposal becomes a liberated metaphor that can continue to be "read forward" into our own situation.[30] According to Ringe:

> Two strands of Israel's tradition come together in Leviticus 25. The first of these is made up of sabbath-year laws (Ex. 21:2–16; 23:10–11; Deut. 15:1–18). . . . The second strand . . . consists of various royal decrees of amnesty or "release" found in the surrounding culture of Mesopotamia as well as in biblical stories (Jer. 34:8–22; Neh. 5:1–13).[31]

Both strands recognize the connection between the worship and confession of God as sovereign and liberator and the obedience to laws requiring social justice. The call for release of slaves, forgiveness of debts, return of the land, and a fallow year for the land stands as a critique of the development of monarchy and accumulation of wealth in Israel, a theme frequently developed in the prophetic tradition.

Isaiah 61:1-2 uses jubilee imagery of release from captivity and good news for the poor to announce God's eschatological reign. This theme in turn finds its way into the heart of the gospel message in the New Testament. It is quoted directly in Luke 4:18-19 and Matthew 11:6/Luke 7:23, and the image of Jesus as the anointed messenger of God's reign is abundantly present in the Synoptic Gospels.[32] Thus the memory of exodus and of a creation where there is community and wholeness points us toward the expectation that the will of God will be done "on earth as it is in heaven" (Matt. 6:10). According to Ringe, this memory of the future is not one of God's sovereignty as a form of hierarchy or domination. Rather, it remembers a tradition in which God as sovereign initiates a covenant partnership with humankind and seeks out ways of establishing a responsible relationship.[33] Indeed the jubilee imagery is not so different from that of God's *oikos*. It evokes God's authority on behalf of all the outcasts of the social household as well as on behalf of creation itself. As Jürgen Moltmann puts it:

> The embodiment of the messianic promises to the poor and the quintessence of the hopes of the alienated is that the world should be "home." This means being at home in existence—that the relationships between God, human beings, and nature lose their tension and are resolved into peace and repose.[34]

When the Messiah comes to break down the walls that separate us, "the world becomes an open house."[35]

2

Paradigms
of Authority

As I noted in chapter 1, an appeal to experience is a crucial part of the methodology in feminist and liberation theologies. The reason for this is that in our modern world of change and pluralism different people see and name their world differently. Theological method needs to take this diversity into account, so that the perspectives of those who have not been heard begin to enrich our reflections. Different persons and groups may see reality differently because of dissimilarities in culture and life experience.

A few years ago I traveled to Korea and Japan to give lectures in feminist theology. Stopping off in Honolulu to visit Pearl Harbor, I entered into the spirit of the War Memorial, seeing the infamy of the Japanese attack and the heroism of the United States in fighting for democracy. Later I traveled with a Japanese friend to Hiroshima and entered into the spirit of the Peace Park, talking to the survivors and seeing the infamy of atomic radiation that still continues to take its deadly toll. These were two pictures of the same difficult reality. In both cases war was hell, but the experience of the war and the way we saw it was "standpoint dependent."[1]

If this is true of recent world history, how much more is it true of the way we read the Bible and understand the Christian tradition? What we hear, understand, and live by depends on our "standpoint" in culture, language, class, age, race, sex, sexual orientation, religious affiliation, and so on. These and other variables affect the particular framework we use for understanding how God is present with us in our lives and how we will respond to that presence through praise and service. Because these frameworks, or paradigms, are so crucial to understanding, I want to look more carefully at the feminist appeal to past and present experience before moving on to propose a different paradigm and a different metaphor for understanding authority in a feminist perspective.

Authority of Experience

When scholars begin their theological investigation by appealing to experience as one source of authority for their interpretation, they are not just referring to their own personal experience. Their initial focus is not on individual experiences but on a social insight drawn from sociology of knowledge. This insight is that our understanding of reality is socially constructed.[2] As James Cone has said:

> We cannot afford to do theology unrelated to human existence. We cannot be "objective," but must recognize with Imamu Baraka that "there is no objective anything"—least of all theology.[3]

This leads Cone to develop black theology out of the socioreligious experience of Blacks. It leads Gustavo Gutiérrez to develop Latin American liberation theology out of the experience of oppressed people in Peru and elsewhere in Latin America.[4] A white feminist theologian like Rosemary Ruether appeals most frequently to white women's experience in the construction of feminist theology and finds it very important to be in dialogue with women of color and of different classes and cultures, in order for feminist theology to advocate full humanity for all women.[5]

Standpoint dependent. The initial claim of feminist and liberation theologians is that the "standpoint dependent" nature of their theologies is no different from any other theology. Every theology is a construction of particular persons and faith communities who confess their faith in God in a language, metaphor, and thought pattern appropriate to that context. John Calvin was very much influenced by his context and the controversies of Geneva and the Continental Reformation. Karl Barth took up the theological tasks involved with a world in the grip of fascism and war. The Barmen Declaration, like other creedal statements in church history, addressed a particular context. In that context the Declaration gave an account of the hope that was in the German confessing community at a particular time and place. Feminist and liberation theologies refuse to hide their so-called "bias" in the name of the universalism of theological ideas. In this way the religious ideas presented are given a context that helps us to understand and to evaluate them.

In appealing to experience, feminist and liberation theologians are also not falling into the false dichotomy between *changeless* truth and purely relative and *changing* truth. Concern for context is not just a popular appeal to the idea that everything is *relative* and nothing really matters. Rather, it is an attempt to deepen and correct our vision of God's promise by understanding that everything is *related*. Because our understanding is related to our context, it matters a great deal who asks the questions and which believing community is struggling with the answers. As Robert McAfee Brown has put it:

> The gospel viewpoint is eternal, but enfleshed. We are enfleshed, but our viewpoint is not eternal; it is mediated through "earthen vessels."

"Jesus Christ is the same yesterday and today and for ever" (Heb. 13:8). But those who receive and transmit the story "have this treasure in earthen vessels" (2 Cor. 4:7).[6]

Having made the claim that all theology is rooted in the experience of particular theologians and communities, the feminist and liberation theologians make a second claim, that the experience of "non-persons" is important to understanding what God is about in the world today. They understand remarks like "She's just a woman," "Why, he never even went to college," and "She can't even speak good English" as indications of a prejudice that may screen out what may be an important word from God. The experience of women is just as important as that of men. It is only considered trivial and of no importance because those who shape ideas and formulate theology consider the work of the wives and servants who care for their needs to be less important than their own work. The theological establishment often seems to live in the world of Aristotle, where women did not count because "by nature" they were not to be allowed to participate in the public arena of life.

The third contention about experience as a source of authority for theology is that this more inductive approach to theology is no less logical or less scientific than other theologies. There is plenty of nonsense in all theologies; no one has a corner on that! But insofar as scholars work to clarify their methods and proceed in a logical and consistent way, there is no reason that the model for logic needs to be taken from philosophy or science rather than from sociology or art and literature. The form of contemporary white male theologies has been developed in answer to the "cultured despisers" of the modern intellectual Western world, but, as Gutiérrez has made very clear, there is every bit as much urgency to address the interpretation of the gospel to the "non-persons" of society as to the "nonbelievers."[7] There is even ample precedent for "enfleshment" of the gospel among the so-called least of our sisters and brothers (Matt. 25:41).

Attention to context. In doing theology with particular attention to context, the experiences and stories of very diverse peoples are not considered a threat to the gospel but, rather, an invitation to expand our understanding of how God's Word is believed and lived out in many different societies and in many different parts of the world. For instance, the recognition that I am doing white feminist theology from a middle-class North American context does not limit my theology. Rather, it situates it so that black, Hispanic, or Asian feminist theologians can give an account of their own hope without feeling that they must compete on some "hit parade" of theologies. The same would be true for other theologies by men and women of other colors, classes, and countries.

The appeal to experience, then, is an invitation to Christians to look at how faith is shaped by life and how it can grow, change, and deepen as the contexts of life and learning shift. The word "context" comes from the Latin word *texto* (to weave or join together). By looking at the context or *surrounding textual material* in the scriptures or other documents of the church, we are often able to gain a new insight into what a particular text means. By studying the *historical circumstances* or events that led to the formation of a particular message in the Bible, a church creed, or some other document, we can better understand what it was intended to say. By looking at the *contemporary circumstances* of our own lives and those of others who are very different from us, we come to understand how we all are one in Christ Jesus yet all express Christ's presence in our lives in different ways. The weaving of life experience into the fabric of our faith is well worth the risks involved in exposing ourselves to unaccustomed partners in Christ.

The experience that becomes a base for feminist and liberation theologies is more than just the occurrences of daily life. The fabric of life is taken seriously and provides a cultural base for the work, but the experience out of which the new theologies are shaped is that of those struggling for full human personhood and dignity and reflecting critically upon their struggle. Out of communities of struggle that are acting for justice, freedom, and peace come critical analysis and new insight that provide a lens of experience through which to understand the gospel message. In the case of feminist theologies, the appeal to woman's experience is not just to the experience of white women or of poor women or of Hispanic women. Rather, it is to the experience of each particular group of women as it is reflected upon critically by those who are struggling for the full participation of women in all the structures of church and society.[8]

Experience is by no means the only source for Christian theology. But neither is it simply an added-on afterthought, when we have finished with careful and reasoned analysis of biblical and church tradition. What happens, for instance, when feminist theologies listen carefully to the critically reflected experiences of women struggling for freedom, is that their way of seeing the world shifts. And as one's standpoint shifts, a new interpretive framework or paradigm develops. In the case of feminists, both men and women, this paradigm has shifted away from the prevailing one of domination toward a paradigm of partnership.

Shifting Paradigms

As Sallie McFague has shown in her book *Metaphorical Theology*, paradigms—interpretive frameworks for understanding reality—provide total contexts for interpretation or meaning and are very slow to change.[9] Each time there is a paradigm shift in the field of theology, much earlier theological understanding continues, yet there is a new understanding of that which evokes consent of faith and action. Each theological shift involves a change in what counts as authoritative in the tradition. Along with liberation theologies, feminist theologies have signaled the beginning of such a paradigm shift that affects all the authority structures in religion and society, including the claim that scripture evokes our consent to faith and action.[10]

The prevailing paradigm of authority in Christian and Jewish religion is one of authority as domination. In this framework all questions of authority are settled with reference to who is number one on the hit parade of authority, so that the person with the highest rank retains control. But as the feminist/liberation paradigm of authority in community begins to become the one most credible to women and men of faith, a new framework emerges that allows for multiple authorities to enrich, rather than to outrank, one another.

Authority as domination. The paradigm that no longer makes sense to feminists is that of authority as domination. This constellation of beliefs, values, and methods shared as a common perspective tends to predominate in church and university and in most theological research and dialogue.[11] Consciously or unconsciously, reality is seen in the form of a hierarchy or pyramid. In feminist theory this paradigm is called "patriarchy." For instance, in her book *Bread Not Stone*, Elisabeth Fiorenza says:

> *Patriarchy* as a male pyramid of graded subordinations and exploitations specifies women's oppression in terms of the class, race, country, or religion of the men to whom we "belong."[12]

This wider meaning of patriarchy is descriptive of every form of exploitation, not just sexism. It refers to the way a society functions, not simply to particular actions of men in society.

In this understanding of authority as domination, things are assigned a divine order, with God at the top, men next, and so on down to dogs, plants, and "impersonal" nature. Theological "truth" is sought through ordering the hierarchy of doctrines, orders, and degrees. The difficulty for women and third-world groups is that their perspectives often do not fit in the pyramid structures of such a system of interpretation. The price of inclusion in the theological enterprise is loss of their own perspective and culture in order to do "good theology" as defined by "those at the top." Anyone who persists in raising questions and perspectives that do not fit the paradigm pays the price of further marginalization. The extreme form of this is the emergence of "heretical groups," who are forced out of the theological conversation and thus lose the possibility of mutual development and critique.

This paradigm of reality is an inadequate theological perspective because it provides a religious rationale for the domination and oppression of the weak by the political, economic, and religious power elites. Such a view is clearly contrary to the prophetic-messianic promise of God's welcome to all the outsiders (Luke 4:16–30). It is also an inadequate paradigm of authority in a world that is so diverse that it no longer makes sense to try to get people into such a rigid view of theological and social truth. Last, it discourages cooperation in the search for meaning because it frames discussion as a competition of ideas in which all participants aim at gaining the "top spot" and vanquishing the others.

Authority as partnership. The emerging feminist paradigm that tries to make sense of biblical and theological truth claims is that of authority as partnership or community. In this view, reality is interpreted in the form of a circle of interdependence. Ordering is explored through inclusion of diversity in a rainbow spectrum that does not require that persons submit to the "top," but rather that they participate in the common task of creating an interdependent community of humanity and nature. Authority is exercised *in* community and not *over* community and tends to reinforce ideas of cooperation, with contributions from a wide diversity of persons enriching the whole. When difference is valued and respected, those who have found themselves marginal to church and society begin to discover their own worth as human beings.

In feminist theory this paradigm has a variety of designations, including partnership, friendship, community, relationship, mutuality, and matriarchy. But in each case, as Elisabeth Moltmann-Wendel has pointed out, the intention is not simply to reverse the old paradigm of domination, but rather to search out an alternative way of ordering our reality and our world that is less harmful to human beings, to nature, and to all creation.[13] This paradigm of reality is not just a romantic dream, because many persons, including feminists, are trying to act out of this perspective. In fact, it is the most realistic alternative possible in a world bent on self-destruction so that some nation or group may claim "victory."

Authority as partnership also begins to provide a theological perspective that seeks to discover a more inclusive consensus on theological issues. This is, perhaps, not unlike the meaning of consensus in the early Christian community: a consensus in the shared story of God's love in Jesus Christ rather than in doctrine (Phil. 2:1–2). It no longer tries to get all persons to accept one neat priority system for theological truth but, rather, welcomes all who are willing to share in building a community of human wholeness that is inclusive of women and men of every race and class. Authority as partnership frames discussion in terms of communal search and sharing in which all can rejoice when anyone gains a new insight that can be shared together on the journey toward God's new creation.

In trying to depict the way in which authority as partnership would function I have often made use of the image of the *rainbow*. In contrast to hierarchical order, imaged by the pyramid of authority as domination, rainbow order consists of a wider variety of colors, and it gains in beauty as more of the color and more of the entire circle may be seen. The rainbow appears most often in the midst of a storm, and this is appropriate for portraying a new reality in the midst of struggling with the old. The rainbow is also a familiar sign to us of God's covenant with creation after the flood (Gen. 9:12–13). Like light hitting a prism, the diverse parts of God's creation refract off each other, creating a synergetic spirit-filled effect of more color, energy, and power. As in God's intention for creation, all parts are welcome to participate as long as they are willing to work for God's covenant purpose of justice, shalom, and what Katharine Sakenfeld calls "loyalty."[14] In rainbow perspective, human beings are no longer imaged at the pinnacle of the pyramid of creation but in the midst of the circle of creation, serving as the housekeepers of what Martin Luther King, Jr., called God's "world house."

> We have inherited a large house, a great "world house" in which we have to live together—black and white, Easterner and Westerner, Gentile and Jew, Catholic and Protestant, Moslem and Hindu—a family unduly separated in ideas, culture, and interest, who, because we can never again live apart, must learn to live with each other in peace.[15]

Household Metaphors

The image of the rainbow is important for helping us begin now to live as a world family in anticipation of God's promised future of mended creation. But rainbows are fleeting images at best, which appear through clouds in the sky, through a sunlit prism on a wall, or on countless commercial products, especially those for little girls! In this commercial form they are carrying the hidden message that women are to live through their dreams of "somewhere over the rainbow," leaving the men to take care of running the "real world." Therefore, we need a metaphor that speaks concretely of human relationships of authority and reminds us that we all do live together in God's house. Such a metaphor might help us understand how we can order our own social and personal relationships in patterns of partnership.

God's presence. Providing metaphors that can picture the way God's presence may be known among us is an important task of theologians. When we think and talk about God we always use metaphors, because God's self-revelation is known to us through our "earthen vessels" of experience. Like the extended metaphors or parables used by Jesus to describe the way God's rule is both like and unlike our human reality, other religious metaphors help us to see how God is like—and unlike—a shepherd, a housekeeper, a father, a mother hen, and so on. In his book *Theological Imagination*, Gordon Kaufman has described this metaphorical aspect of God-talk as the primary work of theology. He writes:

> I have become persuaded that theology is (and always has been) essentially a constructive work of the human imagination, an expression of the imagination's activity helping to provide orientation for human life through developing a symbolical "picture" of the world roundabout and of the human place within that world.[16]

A paradigm is a framework for organizing ideas in a particular field of investigation that defines the issues considered and the methods, questions, and answers likely to be used.[17] A metaphor, on the other hand, is an imaginative way of describing what is still unknown by using an example from present concrete reality. To say "I live in the 'Master's house' " is to provide a metaphorical description of one's position of subordination drawn from the concrete experience of women, servants, and children in many, many houses. To say "I live in a 'household of freedom' " is to use a metaphorical description of one's freedom to participate with others in a community of mutual caring, drawn from the concrete experience of the slaves living in Pharaoh's "house of bondage" and then moving out as the people of God toward a new "house of freedom."

As I indicated in chapter 1, "house of freedom" is a metaphor that may help us understand how authority of partnership can take shape in our lives as an "aperitif" or first taste of the full mending of God's creation. If we are to embrace gladly the diversity of the rainbow and celebrate the differences of those who are our neighbors, we need to function as partners together in a *household of freedom*. It seems to me that this is a particularly good metaphor for authority because it includes a new liberating dimension along with many ancient prototypes of human habitation. We human beings cannot even grow up to understand who we are without companionship and care. Through being partnered by others we learn to become human beings able to partner others, God, the world, and ourselves. Created by God to live in community, we find ourselves in need of some form of human household to sustain life itself.

The importance of the household to the biblical tradition is apparent in the story of a particular human family of Israel, as well as those who were grafted onto that family of faith through the life, death, and resurrection of Jesus Christ. The word for house, dwelling, or temple (*bayith*) is one of the fifty most frequently used words in Hebrew scriptures. Together with the Greek translations (*oikos, oikia*) it appears some two thousand times in the Bible.[18] In the New Testament, house or household becomes a key metaphor for Christ's resurrected body and for the church as the household of faith. The house church and the social structures of the early Christian church form one of the areas of intense research in New Testament scholarship at this time. For instance, John Koenig's study of New Testament hospitality focuses around sharing food and talk at table.[19] And Elisabeth Fiorenza's work *In*

Memory of Her has a particular interest in the "discipleship of equals" and in the later breakdown of that equality as imaged in the "household rules" of Ephesians 5 and 6.[20]

Like the metaphor of "land" so carefully described by Walter Brueggemann as a theme of biblical theology, the metaphor of "household or home" can be a prism for understanding the jubilee promise of human liberation and reconciliation. In fact it is just this metaphor that Brueggemann uses to describe the land histories of Israel. He tells us:

> The first is a history of risking homelessness which yields the gift of home. The second is the deep yearning for home, but in ways which result in homelessness. And in the third history, from exile to Jerusalem we learn that Jesus' embrace of homelessness (crucifixion) is finally the awesome, amazing gift of home (resurrection).[21]

This particular household metaphor for authority is one of *freedom* because it images a community where God's eschatological promise, described in Galatians 3:28, is beginning to happen. When the gifts of God's love are present in a household, all are welcomed as partners, no matter what their differences. Such liberating gifts of God's jubilee are already beginning to be present, as the patriarchal households of Hebrew and Hellenistic traditions are transformed by the presence of Christ.[22] Here freedom is no longer to be exercised as unrestricted domination and control over all who might limit one's freedom by their needs. Rather, it is coming to be exercised as unrestricted partnership, or *koinōnia*, among persons who find the possibility of this new relationship through the gift of God's love.[23]

New households. The new households we glimpse occasionally in the New Testament provide us with some clues about how authority would function in a household of freedom. In the Gospels the women and men gathered in the movement around Jesus formed a new community of those who did God's will (Matt. 10:37; 12:48–49). As Luise Schottroff has pointed out, those who followed Jesus became a new *family of God*, and this was very good news for them.[24] These followers were the *ochlos*, the poor and the outcasts of society. It may be the case that they were so marginal that their families were broken down and both women and men were forced to move from place to place seeking food and work like the laborers in the vineyard who were hired in the last hour. That parable presents what was probably a familiar scene of workers waiting all day for work and willing to work even one hour without asking about the wages, just hoping that they might get something to eat (Matt. 20:1–16). Certainly the message of Jesus could lead to division among families, but for many it provided a new family household when their own family had already been broken up by the economic conditions of their time.[25]

In the Hellenistic setting of the Pauline congregations, the resurrection communities often seem to have met in households. But they were distinctly unlike the basic political unit of that society, which included family, slaves, freed persons, servants, laborers, business associates, and tenants. Instead, the house churches seem to have been more like the voluntary associations of Hellenistic society that provided hospitality and support. With a few women and men of higher social status who sometimes served as patrons of these associations, the majority were people of lower status, as Paul acknowledges in 1 Corinthians 1:26–30.[26] These people were no longer under the control of the patriarch. They were a new *koinōnia* often gathered in a home, but now containing women and men working in ministry as partners, with slaves, freed persons, and servants sharing in the new household of freedom.

Many of the details of this pattern are still under debate among New Testament scholars, but there is consensus that such a social pattern is glimpsed in Paul's writings, and that the later writings of the New Testament reveal a gradual accommodation to the old patriarchal patterns both in the home and in the church. Although Christians would not worship Caesar as head of the religious family, they sought to prove that in everything else they were loyal citizens (1 Peter 2:13–17). Thus Ephesians 5:21–6:9 appeals to a household order of subordination of wife, child, slave to the husband, father, master. The church is now called the *household of God* in both its local and universal manifestations and begins to develop orders of ministry that are hierarchical (1 Tim. 3:15; 1 Peter 2:5).[27]

These New Testament prototypes of household help us to glimpse some images of what a household might be like. Another passage from the New Testament that seems particularly helpful to me in spelling out what the household of freedom might look like is Paul's advice about living *hōs mē* (as if not) in 1 Corinthians 7. Here Paul advises the church in Corinth concerning marriage and celibacy. In verses 29 and 30 Paul advises the brothers and sisters in Christ to

> let those who are married live as though they were not,
> and those who mourn as though they were not mourning,

and those who rejoice as though they were not rejoicing,
and those who buy as though they had no goods,
and those who deal with the world as though they had
no dealings with it.[28]

Although our eschatology may not be the same as that of Paul, he still provides us with a clue about living together in freedom. The clue is that because of our commitment to live as if God's new creation were already in our midst, we understand all social roles and relationships as secondary or penultimate. Our relationship to God is ultimate, and therefore all other social roles and hierarchies are no longer of ultimate importance. This does not mean that such human relationships do not matter, but rather that they are refocused because of Christ's gift of freedom (Gal. 5:1). Our relationships matter very much just because the way we live out those relationships of loyalty, shalom, and justice is an expression of what matters ultimately in our lives.

I myself am so partial to the idea of living "as if not" that I named my house Hos Me. Of course, I intended to live in the house as if the bank did not own it! But I also wanted to live in the house as if I did not own it. That is, I wanted to recognize that this treasured possession should not come between me and the needs of my neighbor or the call of God. One day I received a plaque as a housewarming present which had the house name written in Hebrew letters. Since then, even the name is "as if not" because no one can read it. *Hōs Mē* is Greek and not Hebrew, and you cannot make any sense out of a sign that says *hōs mē* in Hebrew letters. That is, you can't make sense of it unless you are a Hebrew scholar. One day, one of my colleagues, Bonnie Kittel, visited me and looked at the plaque. She announced that as far as she could tell it was supposed to be some sort of transliteration in Hebrew letters of the words "my house"! It *is* my house, but a whole lot more, and I would like it to become part of God's wider household of freedom.

When our relationship to God is what matters ultimately, we can dare to live in patterns other than those provided by the customs and traditions of our own culture. Many of these traditions render "household" an ambiguous term. There is the Greek tradition of the patriarchal household separate from public life but still constituted as "man's castle." There is also the tradition of the household of God, in which the church of the fathers came to replace the early egalitarian house church. Ultimately those in this church household would no longer live "as if not" but, rather, as the servant of Constantine and Caesar's household.

At the same time, however, the household in all its many varieties is understood in every culture as a place where human life is to be nurtured, and it is the place where women and children feel at home. Any feminist theology that is not concerned with what happens in the home and family will fail to re-picture the area of life that is most important to women. For instance, speaking of black women, Delores Williams has said that black female liberation and black family liberation are inseparable. One of the tasks of feminist theology is the construction of critical principles of biblical interpretation that will constitute a word of hope for those on the underside.[29]

If there were a household of freedom, those who dwelt in it could find a way to nurture life without paying the price of being locked into roles of permanent domination and subordination. That is what makes this particular metaphor so powerful. The term "household" surprises us as a choice of metaphor for authority in partnership because of its oppressive associations. Yet the term "freedom" forces us to use our imagination to see what household could have to do with freedom, both in personal relationships and in the social and political structures of God's world house.[30] In a time and place when the structures of human community are every bit as much in disarray as in the first-century Roman empire, it is time to look into ways that the paradigm of domination can be confronted. With this task in mind, I hope that Hannah Arendt is correct when she says of these latter two centuries that "the eagerness to liberate and to build a new house where freedom can dwell is unprecedented and unequaled in all prior history."[31]

3

Power of Naming

Several years ago I attended a meeting of the Presbytery of
Southern New England in the First Presbyterian Church of Stam-
ford, Connecticut. The church is designed to look like a whale,
with the sanctuary representing a stained-glass version of Jonah's
deep-sea abode. Conducting business in such a dramatic and
vaulted sanctuary was a bit of a problem, but I was looking forward to the final worship service. Two women from Yale Divinity
School had been accepted as candidates for ordination, and they
would be received under care at that time. Finally the service
began and the scripture lesson, Psalm 8, was read in "unexpur-
gated" RSV.

> What is man that thou art mindful of him,
> and the son of man that thou dost care for him?

The preacher ascended the high pulpit to preach while the women
sat below. When it came time for them to be received, the women
knelt on the steps while the "Fathers and Brethren" leading the
service stood above in the chancel. In accordance with the Presbyterian Constitution, women were allowed to prepare for ordination, and female pronouns were prescribed for the reception
liturgy. But what about the power of naming and imaging in that
service? Afterward I joined a few others in a protest to the powers
that be, but I knew that the religious language and symbolism of
the liturgy had reinforced a pervasive and long-lasting model for
divine and human behavior.[1] The religious paradigm of domination was alive and well!

The language and symbolism of domination and subordination
that reinforces patriarchal religious, social, and political institutions is to be found in the Bible as well as in our midst. Psalm 8,

for example, makes it abundantly clear that God and men are the actors on the stage of life, and many liturgical settings continually play this out in the details of person, place, symbol, and language experienced in churches. In most English versions the language of the psalm itself uses male pronouns not only for God but also for humankind. In addition, it reflects an interpretation of Genesis 1 that seems to place God at the top, with males a little lower (hob-nobbing with the angels in the KJV), with power over all other creatures and creation itself. In spite of the beauty of this psalm of praise, its use in worship is problematic for those seeking a new paradigm of partnership. Yet perhaps Psalm 8 can help us see why the issue of God-talk and human talk is crucial for Jewish and Christian feminists who have experienced the power of the writ-ten, acted, and spoken word to mirror and mold their lives.

This power of naming has implications for a feminist under-standing of power and authority in community. Power, as we have seen, is the ability to accomplish desired ends, and the power to name our reality does just that. We have only to look at television or the newspaper to see how the language of word and symbol names everything, from dog food to star wars, that a particular sponsor wishes us to buy. Communications is an industry because naming is a powerful tool for accomplishing the desired ends of the economic, political, and religious rulers of society.

Joined to this power of naming is the reinforcement that comes when those who do the naming are understood as persons with authority or legitimate right to this form of control. Occasionally someone gets "out of hand" with a racist remark or an outright lie, and the authority of the speaker or media is questioned. Yet we are reluctant to question everything we see and hear, to ask about the hidden persuaders seeking to convince us that the poor are lazy cheats, women are sex objects, violence is sexy, AIDS victims are being punished by God, farmers deserve to lose their farms, and third-world people like being exploited. Just by refusing to question what we hear, we are assenting to the authority of those who are naming our world.

As Christians we live under the authority of the Word of God, an authority that tells us quite a different story. Paradoxically, this other story is also in Psalm 8, but we seldom hear it because of the old paradigm operating in our heads. This other equally powerful God-talk of the psalmist is telling us how much God values human persons and exhorting us to give God praise by living out our responsibility of partnership in the care of creation.[2] Before turn-ing to Christian understandings of the authority of the Word, and powerful God-talk, I want to look more closely at the connection of word and power and the importance of language usage in church and society.

Word and Power

Since the eighteenth century, linguists have been aware that language influences the way we think and that language is in turn shaped by the culture of the speakers. The Sapir/Whorf hypothesis about language has had a great deal of effect on twentieth-century studies of language, as linguists tested out this theory that language, culture, and thought are dynamically interrelated.[3] Communications experts are not the only ones who have become aware of the power of language. Groups of people struggling to change the balance of power between black and white, rich and poor, nature and humanity, men and women have discovered that talk is not just talk! Because talk is related to thought and action, talk can *always* hurt you, just like sticks and stones. As Adrienne Rich puts it,

> Language is as real, as tangible in our lives as streets, pipelines, telephone switchboards, microwaves, radioactivity, cloning laboratories, nuclear power stations.[4]

Theft of language. The feminist movement has discovered that naming ourselves has to do with claiming our own identity, thought, and action. Women struggling for equality understand that what Adrienne Rich calls the "theft of language" is part of women's condition of relative powerlessness.[5] Changing sex-exclusive language is no longer some whim of a few fringe women with what one Harvard linguistics professor described as "pronoun envy."[6] It is a serious, well-researched, political action to change sexist language and social structures. The generic "he/man" was a result of the politics of grammarians who convinced the English Parliament to make it a law in 1850 because men should "naturally" take precedence. Now feminists are seeking a return to the earlier usage of generic "they" with the singular noun.[7] Nor are feminists alone in such views. The *Oxford English Dictionary* had already declared the generic "man" obsolete by its 1971 edition. It is no accident that there are more than 1,000 articles listed from 1975 to 1983 in an annotated bibliography on gender in language, while there were only 230 from 1960 to 1975 and 20 from 1900 to 1960.[8] With other oppressed groups, women have discovered that language is powerful, and they take these words from linguist Barrie Thorne very seriously:

The social consequences of a language—in daily use by hundreds of millions of people—which tends to deprecate or ignore a whole class of human beings, and to set them apart by their usage, are devastating.[9]

Even the basic dictionary meanings of power and of language reveal that they have something to do with each other. In most dictionaries the first definition of power describes it as domination. Although it is obvious, at least to feminist thinkers, that power can be exercised as empowerment, so as to enhance the power of others, in social interactions it is usually assumed to be power *over* others.[10]

As we have already seen, an extremely important form of social control is human language. Elites of any society not only set the norms for language, they usually control the resources for education and communication, and therefore they possess the power to describe the social and natural world and to assign a place to different sexes, races, classes, and species.[11]

Although the Latin root indicates that the word refers to use of the tongue and to patterns of speech in a particular cultural group, human language is more accurately understood as the signs, images, sounds, gestures, marks, and expressions used to communicate ideas and feelings. Such communication is an essential part of human nature and provides the metaphors of thought, as well as the means of establishing relationships with others and discovering personal identity in communal relationships. Through communication with others we learn to name or assign meaning to the world around us and to name ourselves as part of that world.

In considering the "theft of language" and the consequent power of naming, claiming, and changing reality, it is important to remember the wide variety in forms of communication.[12] Otherwise we assume that relationships are established only through spoken or written language and ignore other forms of communication that also "speak" to persons without extensive schooling or linguistic training. Often women and marginal groups in society lose the power of communication because the way they relate to others is not recognized by the dominant groups. As Margaret Miles points out in her visual history of Western culture,

the lives of non-language users were no less ordered by ideas and images than were those of language users. To dismiss their lives as uninteresting for historical understanding is the judgment of an educationally privileged elite that reflects an exclusive interest in the antecedents of modern subjective consciousness.[13]

Power and language. The interrelation of power and language is already clearly evident in the two versions of creation in Genesis 1 and 2. In Genesis 1:28 God gives male and female human beings dominion over all creatures as stewards of the earth. In Genesis 2:19 the earth creature "calls the name" of every living creature to underscore the subordination of the animal world to the earth creature. According to Phyllis Trible, the naming formula is not used in 2:23, when the man expresses joy in the creation of woman as an equal partner.[14] Only later, in Genesis 3:20, does the naming formula of subordination appear, in conjunction with the fall. Here the woman is named Eve, mother of all living. She is to bring life into a household ruled over by her husband.

Power determines the way language is used, because those who are able to carry out their intent do so in regard to human communication as well as other matters. At the same time, language itself is a powerful force in establishing positions of domination and subordination and in legitimating authority. The way in which networks of power and language interlock in society is described by Elizabeth Janeway in *Powers of the Weak:*

> Ordered power operates within society as a gravitational force that holds us together. Like language, it is a network that reaches everywhere and touches us all. If language is the technique by which we communicate with each other, power is the process by which we interact in order to implement the plans that we have made.[15]

A good example of the power of language to reflect the status quo in our society is the story of the Revised Standard Version of the Bible and the struggles of the National Council of the Churches of Christ and its Division of Education and Ministry to "provide leadership and resources that support and facilitate the church as a Biblically informed community of faith and action."[16] The RSV translation committee and the Inclusive-Language Lectionary Committee intended to provide such scholarly resources. But in both cases the resistance to change of language and thought patterns seems to have reflected a fear of social and religious change. There were those who burned copies of the RSV New Testament when it was issued in 1946, as well as persons who sent hate mail and threats when *An Inclusive-Language Lectionary*, based on the RSV, appeared in 1983.

The writings in the Bible took shape in a variety of cultures, but they were all patriarchal, and it is not possible either to expect or desire the original manuscripts to reflect sex-inclusive language. Yet it is important that translations be as accurate as possible in conveying the sense of the message in contemporary speech. It is equally important that inclusive versions of the Bible be available for those who wish to convey the message that God's love is offered to women and men alike, and especially to all those traditionally excluded from social and religious communities through language and social usage.

Authority of the Word

There is nothing new about the debate over scriptural literalism and interpretation. Nor is there anything new about the need to reinterpret and retranslate the Bible as often as cultures and languages change. Only in this way can the Word be heard in new situations and contexts. What is new is that a growing number of women and men, struggling to free themselves and others from structures of oppression, include the insights of that struggle as part of the criteria of what constitutes authority in the Christian church.

According to David Kelsey's analysis, the Bible comes to make sense in communities of faith not through the literal reading of the text but through an "imaginative construal" or interpretive framework that evokes our consent and thus becomes authoritative for the way we would live out our faith.[17] Kelsey is referring to the more narrow understanding of paradigm as a model for interpretation within a community of discourse. As Thomas Kuhn has pointed out, paradigms function both as general social worldviews, like the contrasting views of patriarchy and partnership, and as specific models of research, such as those used by different theologians to explain the meaning of biblical authority.[18]

Scripture functions authoritatively in faith communities whose model or paradigm for understanding God's presence includes the claim that God is to be known through the story of liberation and salvation that is told in the Hebrew and Christian scriptures. But different communities stress one aspect of this story more than others. There are many ways of construing the meaning of God's presence, as the existence of Roman Catholic sacramental theology, Reformed theology of the Word, Quaker theology of the Spirit, and many more theological frameworks will attest. Nevertheless, according to Kelsey, the construction of a Christian theological framework or paradigm has three limits if it is to be recognized within the Christian tradition as an authoritative interpretation of scripture. It must be a reasoned and intelligible form of discourse, it must make use of the structure of Christian tradition and biblical interpretation, and it must speak of what is "seriously imaginable" in a particular time and place.[19]

Feminist interpretations. Feminist interpretations vary a great deal and are strongly rooted in the particular faith communities of the interpreters as they struggle with these criteria and ask if they indeed still count as evoking consent in a Christian theological paradigm of partnership. The interpreters certainly do seek to be *intelligible*, reasoned, and logical. However, as we say in the discussion of paradigms, their struggles with abstract hierarchical thought and language patterns have led many women and men to insist that methods of interpretation include an inductive process of action and reflection in which a major criterion for consistency is the way that reflection is brought together with actions and concrete experiences.[20]

Feminist interpreters are also *in touch with tradition* and the biblical witness, but they raise radical questions about the unfaithfulness of the church as guardian of that tradition and about the ways scripture and tradition have been used and misused. The question of the trajectory of a tradition as it has shaped the lives of subsequent generations of women and men is considered an important part of reconstruction. Has it helped to harm or heal those who are seeking to live in obedience to God? Traditions for other religions are also studied to find out if their trajectories are more life-giving.

The community of struggle also affects which interpretations feminists entertain as *seriously imaginable*. As Margaret Farley has pointed out, speaking of what is seriously imaginable in the lives of women and other oppressed groups raises questions about whether a God who is sexist, racist, or classist is God at all.[21] For my part, I cannot imagine a God who does not seek to be partner with all humankind in the mending of creation. Therefore, I look at the Bible from the perspective of all those struggling for human wholeness, including this principle of interpretation as part of what is seriously imaginable in the paradigm of authority.

The struggle to interpret the scriptures and to articulate the authority of the Word continues as we seek to remain open to ways God's Spirit may be speaking to us in our communities of faith. But this very brief description of the way certain biblical interpretations come to evoke assent in particular communities of faith and struggle indicates that people's understanding and use of metaphor is directly related to their particular religious community and is not easily dislodged by any amount of logic.

It also indicates that discussion about the appropriate use and interpretation of scripture is founded on the question of one's general paradigm or worldview. What we deem appropriate is directly related to whether we understand God, world, and church according to a fixed pyramid of domination or according to a pluralistic rainbow of partnership. The former leads to a view of authority that tends to guard the Word and to set forth its interpretation through doctrine. The latter leads to a view of authority that tends to incarnate the Word and set forth its interpretation through telling stories of faith and struggle.

Perhaps this description of the function of biblical authority will help us understand that the issue of inclusive language is not so much an issue of words as of the paradigm or framework of interpretation that determines the way people understand their faith and live it out. This is in no way intended to deny that the basis of faith for Christians is the self-revelation of God in Jesus Christ through the continuing power and presence of the Holy Spirit. The foundation of the Christian faith claim is that there is a God who is the source of life and love and that this God has chosen to be known through the spoken and enacted word.

Word of God. Christians often speak of the scriptures as the "Word of God" because it is a source of authority in their lives and actions. God is understood as speaking to the Christian community through the biblical story. But there are several overlapping ways of explaining how this happens. Often people use the term "Word of God" in reference to the Bible as a witness to God's *actions,* and especially to the gospel story of the One whom we call the *Living Word.* Scripture is also understood as God's Word because it has been experienced by people of faith and struggle as *life-giving:* a source of strength, a foundation for their lives. Third, the biblical message is heard as the Word of God when it is inspired by God's Spirit as a *lively word* that shapes life. Finally, in spite of its mixed messages, the Bible is considered trustworthy because Christians trust in God's *loyal word,* or covenant faithfulness, and are willing to wrestle with the texts in order to respond faithfully in their own context of loyalty and obedience. As Phyllis Bird puts it, the scriptures are

> the place where the church hears God speaking and discerns God's presence when their words are studied and pondered and questioned—and opened for us by the Stranger who accompanies us on our journey and breaks bread with us.[22]

None of these understandings of God's Word are inconsistent with the work of feminist interpretation and language changes. The purpose of that work is to allow the biblical message to be heard as God's Word in spite of the patriarchal historical context in which the stories of faith were shaped. In a sense, Christian feminists are constantly admitting that the Bible is "hopelessly sexist" and known to be "harmful to women's health." Yet out of communities of faith and struggle they appeal to God whose authority works through the power of love, against God who rules through the patriarchal power of domination. The desire of those working for inclusive language is not for domination but for true diversity in which no one image or model decides the nature of God or of the human person.

Powerful God-Talk

Many persons believe that changes in the language used to describe God are heresy and that biblical authority rests upon verbal inspiration of the text and a closed canon. This particular interpretation is not necessary to the recognition of the canon of the Bible or of its divine inspiration. According to Phyllis Bird, canon indicates acceptance by the church as authoritative for faith, not the exact number of books. Selection of books in the canon was based on the norm of apostolic witness, rather than on an exclusive claim that the Holy Spirit inspired only these particular writings.[23]

There are persons, however, who include verbal inspiration and closed canon as part of their paradigm of biblical authority, yet find it imperative to make our language about God more inclusive. A good example of this evangelical feminist position is Virginia Ramey Mollenkott's book *The Divine Feminine*.[24] She joins many other women and men who see much of our God-talk or theology as part of a pattern of sexism that reinforces and legitimatizes "father right."[25] As Carol Christ puts it, "God in 'his' heaven is both a model *of* divine existence and a model *for* women's subordination to men."[26]

Of course, theology is never just talking about God. In thinking about God we use our whole self, our language, culture, experience, and tradition, to understand God's self-revelation in and through the world. The way we think about God is affected by every aspect of our lives: our race, age, nationality, sex, sexual orientation, religious and economic background, social groups, and education. When the way we think about God is no longer seriously imaginable in relation to the way we think about ourselves and our world, we experience "cognitive dissonance." If this happens, our theological understanding of God may need to change, if it is not to be ignored or thrown out altogether. Such a struggle can be seen in the story of Celie in Alice Walker's *The*

Color Purple. Toward the end of the novel Celie gets into a discussion with Shug about her image of God as a big white man with a gray beard. Shug replies,

> Ain't no way to read the bible and not think God white, she say. Then she sigh. When I found out I thought God was white, and a man, I lost interest. You mad cause he don't seem to listen to your prayers. Humph! Do the mayor listen to anything colored say?[27]

Alternative metaphors. This is the situation of many women and men today. They do not claim that it is impossible to image God as "a great white Father," but they do claim that this image no longer is powerful God-talk for them and should not be used to reinforce white male power over them. Even those for whom this metaphor for God is not irrelevant or anachronistic are coming to recognize that it can be *idolatrous.* As Sallie McFague points out, the problem is not that God is imaged as Father but that we have made Father the one root-metaphor for Christianity, replacing the message of God's reign with a message of patriarchy.

> It is not just that "God the Father" is a frequent appellation for the divine, but that the entire structure of divine-human and human-human relationship is understood in a patriarchal framework.[28]

Patriarchal reinforcement seems to be the opposite of Jesus' intention in speaking of God as "abba," according to Robert Hamerton-Kelly. He suggests that Jesus' use of "Father" is intended to emphasize the freedom and love of the new family of God's reign in opposition to the existing patriarchal family structures.[29] God transcends all our metaphors, and it is important to avoid a metaphor that has become narrowly identified with patriarchal authority. To use only one and claim it cannot be changed is to fall into idolatry. In our time the search has begun for a variety of metaphors and translations that more closely picture the God of whom the Gospels speak, a God who is at work in the mending of creation through the emptying out of structures of domination and exploitation and the creation of new community (Luke 1:46–55).

This presents difficulties for many people. For instance, in a class on "Feminist Theology and Ethics" at Yale Divinity School, one woman complained about the singing of the Doxology in her local church using the ending "Creator, Son, and Holy Ghost." "If they change 'Father,' why not 'Son'?" she said. "Where can we draw the line?" Indeed, "Son" could have been changed to "Christ" as an indication that the risen Christ transcends sexuality as do all members of the Godhead. And certainly "Holy Ghost" is no longer the preferred translation for "Holy Spirit." But when all is said and done, it is the question itself that presents the greatest barrier to inclusive language and thought.

The woman's question is based on a patriarchal paradigm used to justify the exclusion of those who do not fit into the approved hierarchy of male reality. The patriarchal mind-set decides the truth and draws the line, and suddenly those outside the line become heretics. We know, however, that theological lines are always moving in response to changes in human culture. There are very few clear lines, and it is perhaps better not to pose the question of authority that way. In the Christian faith there is a *center* (commitment to Jesus Christ) and a *circle* (a hermeneutical circle). Every theological interpretation affects every other, so that we continue to move around the circle trying to create metaphors and models that are faithful to the center of our commitment.

The metaphors we use are powerful God-talk, for they determine the way we think about God and about ourselves as men and women, created in God's image. As Gordon Kaufman says, "Conceptual, symbolic, and imagistic elements are each involved in all serious uses of 'God-talk,' and failing to recognize this will impoverish and falsify our understanding."[30]

Christian feminists have not been hesitant in pointing out the abundance of metaphors for God in biblical and church tradition, and in other religions as well. Mary Daly has created an entire new gyn/ecological language for speaking about God.[31] Her work is foundational to an ever-growing number of post-Christian and post-Jewish feminists who find God-talk such a powerful tool of oppression that it must be liberated entirely from male metaphors. Heeding Mary Daly's assertion that "if God is male, then the male is God," they have begun to speak of the Goddess.[32]

Even from within the Christian tradition, feminist theologians have come to recognize the legitimacy of encountering the divine as goddess.[33] An amazing example of this is found in writings of Nelle Morton, a feminist theologian in her eighties. In *The Journey Is Home*, she describes "Goddess as Metaphoric Image."[34] The powerful aspect of Goddess-talk, according to Morton, is that it provides a divine metaphor at once freeing and healing for women as well as men. This talk is not heretical, for it makes no claim that our Creator, Liberator, and Advocate is literally Father or Mother, God or Goddess. It simply addresses itself to the idolatrous power of God-talk that refuses to use any but male metaphors for God, by creating space in our language for God/Goddess to be God.

Other theologians are working to overcome what Daniel Migli-

ore calls "distorted images of divine power," such as the image of
the supreme monarch.[35] In order to underline the importance of a
kenōsis or emptying out of such power, Rosemary Ruether begins
her book *Sexism and God-Talk* with a feminist midrash entitled
"The Kenosis of the Father." Her story portrays the power of the
myth of permanent hierarchy that was so pervasive, even among
Jesus' followers, that God's transformation of power and "self-
emptying" in Jesus Christ was an idea that was hardly even
tried.[36] In pursuit of imagery and language that might represent
this transformation of power for domination to empowerment for
others, I have made use of the metaphor of God as partner, and
other theologians use similar relational metaphors. For instance,
Carter Heyward speaks of God as "power in relation" in her book
The Redemption of God, and Sallie McFague proposes the metaphor of God as "friend" as an alternative to God as "father."[37]

Divine Wisdom.   Another alternative metaphor is that of Sophia or divine Wisdom (*hokhmah* in Hebrew). The understanding
of Wisdom as a female hypostasis or personification of God's active presence in the world developed in response to the religious
contexts of the Jewish diaspora in Egypt, Sumaria, and Babylon
and, later, in the Roman empire.[38] By the first century B.C.E. she
had become a very influential figure in Hellenistic Judaism. According to Joan Chamberlain Engelsman, Sophia was sufficiently
powerful as a divine being that such writers as Philo were determined to repress this aspect of Jewish theology, both by expressing Sophia's preexistent role in creation through the Greek idea of
a male *logos* and by spiritualizing wisdom as a divine figure and
emphasizing her incarnational aspects in human flesh as a female
personification of evil.[39] Nevertheless, Wisdom writings are found
in Hebrew and Christian scriptures in places such as Job 28, Proverbs 1–9, and James. They were also influential in the writing of
Colossians, Ephesians, and John, according to Raymond Brown.[40]
Other Wisdom writings are found in the Apocrypha and the
Pseudepigrapha and include such writings as Sirach, the Wisdom
of Solomon, Baruch, and Enoch.

In her book *In Memory of Her*, Elisabeth Fiorenza emphasizes
the importance of Sophia as an alternative metaphor for God. She
says:

> Divine Sophia is Israel's God in the language and *Gestalt* of the god-
> dess. Sophia is called sister, wife, mother, beloved, and teacher. She
> is the leader on the way, the preacher in Israel, the taskmaster and
> creator God.[41]

In Fiorenza's understanding, the earliest Christian theology is Sophialogy: the interpretation of Jesus as Sophia's messenger or as Sophia herself. Some of the references in the Gospels appear to connect Jesus and Sophia; for instance, the yoke which is easy, in Matthew 11:30, and Jesus as preexistent Wisdom, in John 1:1-14. A similar idea may be behind Paul's identification of Christ as "the power of God and the wisdom of God" (1 Cor. 1:24). Fiorenza finds parallels in early Christian hymns, such as the one in Philippians 2:11 to Enoch 43:1-2.

> Sophia found no place where she might dwell
> Then a dwelling place was assigned her in the heavens
> Wisdom sent forth to make her dwelling
>   among the children of humans
> And found no dwelling place
> Wisdom returned to her place
> And took her seat among the angels.[42]

Some of the Sophia texts that point to the use of Sophia Christology in the early Christian communities are found in what is considered to be a common source (Q) for Matthew and Luke. Analysis of the texts may indicate that Luke has continued the earlier Q tradition that Jesus is a messenger or prophet of Sophia, while Matthew has already made the connection of Jesus with Sophia. For instance, Luke 7:31-35 says that "wisdom is justified by all her children" (John the Baptist and Jesus), whereas the parallel in Matthew 11:16-19 says that "wisdom is justified by her deeds" (the healings and preaching of good news) that John the Baptist hears about in prison. In Matthew 23:37-39 and Luke 12:34-35, a similar shift in emphasis may be seen. Verses 34-36 in Matthew seem to indicate that Jesus is Sophia, the mother hen who would have gathered Jerusalem's children under her wings but finds her prophets rejected, while Luke implies that Jesus himself is one of Wisdom's rejected prophets (Luke 11:49-51; cf. 19:41-44; 2 Esdras 1:28-32).[43]

The Gospel of John shows an even more complete integration of Sophialogy into Christology, with Jesus presented in the form of the "I am" Wisdom sayings and identified with the personified divine Wisdom, now identified with the preexistent logos. Raymond Brown writes that

> the Prologue brings together strains from both the Prophetic and the Wisdom Literature of the OT. The title, "the Word," is closer to the prophetic "word of the Lord"; but the description of the activity of the Word is very much like that of Wisdom.[44]

I am sure that the details of the trajectory of the Sophia tradition and of the female personification of God's presence among the people will be argued for some time to come. There is still much discussion of the divine status of Sophia and her relationship to Yahweh in the Hebrew tradition and to Jesus and the Spirit in New Testament tradition. Yet there is no doubt that Sophia provides an alternative female metaphor for God at the center of Jewish and Christian tradition. This metaphor conveys a combination of strong public prophetic action on behalf of justice for the outcasts of society, as well as strong love, loyalty, and caring. These are not separated in the gospel message of Jesus and of God's new household, and they should not be separated in our own images of God or of ourselves.

Like the jubilee tradition discussed in chapter 1, the Sophia tradition has been "read forward" into the New Testament and the life of the early church. In fact we are able to say of it what Sharon Ringe says of jubilee:

> The power of these images to help us say what it means to confess Jesus as the Christ, as well as to confront our assumptions concerning values and priorities in our daily lives, becomes a vehicle by which we read forward or interpret from the biblical traditions into our own situation.[45]

The household imagery in the Sophia tradition reminds us again of the long trajectory of the image of God's dwelling with us as One who cares for the world house and calls us to share in the knowledge of righteousness (Ps. 90:1–2). Thus in Proverbs 9:1–6 we read:

Wisdom has built her house, she has set up her seven pillars.
She has slaughtered her beasts, she has mixed her wine,
     she has also set her table.
She has sent out her maids to call from the highest places in the town,
"Whoever is simple, let [them] turn in here!"
To [those who are] without sense she says,
"Come, eat of my bread and drink of the wine I have mixed.
Leave simpleness, and live, and walk in the way of insight."

Of the many possible biblical metaphors for God, I find the metaphor of *God as housekeeper* (the *oikonomos*) particularly helpful as I try to reconstruct the house of authority. Like Sophia, who issues her call to the banquet from "the highest places in the town," and like the woman searching high and low for the lost coin, God continues to search throughout her world house (the *oikoumenē*) looking for all the outcasts and lost persons of society and rejoicing when they are found (Luke 15:8–10; 14:15–24).[46] Her divine economy (*oikonomia*) is one of breaking across the barriers of language and culture so that we may one day be restored in the Spirit as one household of God (Eph. 1:10; 2:13–22). This is powerful God-talk, which may provide us with language and metaphor equipped for the building up (*oikodomē*) of the household of freedom.

4

New House
of Authority

In the introduction to this book, I spoke of the "feminist touch." In a manner similar to the Midas touch of gold, everything feminists touch in a patriarchal society seems to turn into a question of authority. Because we live in a society where authority is understood as legitimate domination by those who have social, political, economic, and ecclesial power, those who step out of their subordinate place in the pyramid are uppity, to say the least! Nowhere is the feminist touch more evident than in the area of scripture and tradition, for here the religious authorities have frequently sanctioned a hierarchical way of life designed to legitimate "father right" rather than human rights.[1] New interpretations of tradition are often exciting and yield new insights for living faithfully as Christians, but they cause both anger and fear among those who find security in the old house of authority.

A particularly painful example of this fear may be seen in the 1984 decision of the Southern Baptist Convention that the "order of authority" (God, Christ, man, woman) excludes women from pastoral leadership. God requires their submission "because the man was first in creation and the woman first in the Edenic fall" (1 Tim. 2:11–14).[2] Women not only cannot be ordained, they are cursed by God with permanent subordination because of their primary responsibility for *everyone's* sin! Even grace seems of no avail for those whose very nature threatens the old male house of authority.

Those who wish to protect this old house are, perhaps, well advised to reject women as pastoral leaders, because there are a great many persons in many different confessional houses that are becoming "house revolutionaries."[3] Women and men are searching out ways of understanding the Bible and the Jewish and Christian traditions from the perspective of the losers, in the struggle for full human equality and participation in the life of the people of God. They do not abandon their traditions; rather, they claim them as their own. The biblical witness continues to evoke consent and to be pondered as a word of life, yet many of the teachings as well as the patriarchal context of the ancient world are rejected. As Mary Ann Tolbert has pointed out in her article in *The Bible and Feminist Hermeneutics*, feminist biblical scholarship is profoundly paradoxical because "one must struggle against God as enemy assisted by God as helper, or one must defeat the Bible as patriarchal authority by using the Bible as liberator."[4] For myself, I continue to live with this paradox, because the Bible still helps to make sense of who I am as a woman of faith and because the biblical witness opens the way to a future that will be so radically different from the present that it will be called "new" (Rev. 21:1–4).

Living in the Master's House

As Christian women and men we are all very much caught up in this paradox. We continue to dwell in the old house of authority, the master's house, while at the same time seeking to understand just how Jesus cleansed that religious house so that it could become "a house of prayer for all the nations" (Mark 11:17). One way to work on "temple cleansing" is to reformulate each text and doctrine with great scholarly care. This reformulation is crucial to the preaching of the gospel, but it is my contention that more than that is needed. This is why I emphasized the importance of a paradigm shift in chapter 2, a conversion experience in which we no longer see the world in the same way as before. I want to take Paul's advice in 2 Corinthians 5:16–17 to heart:

> From now on, therefore, we regard no one from a human point of view; even though we once regarded Christ from a human point of view, we regard Christ thus no longer. Therefore, if any one is in Christ, there is a new creation; the old has passed away, behold, the new has come.

When we work at things piece by piece, we do not necessarily change the structures of thought used for interpretation, preaching, and Christian life. It is a little like trying to win at *Monopoly* when you just own Baltic Avenue, without any hotels! The only possibility of winning in such circumstances is by changing the rules of the game. If the rules say that property owners should collect rents and distribute them equally, then perhaps everyone would be able to continue in the game and there would be no more losers. In the same way our paradigm of authority needs to change. If authority is understood as *authorizing* the inclusion of all persons as partners, and power is understood as *empowerment* for self-actualization together with others, then the entire game of authority shifts, not just the separate pieces of property and hotels called Bible and traditions.

In this perspective the question of women's ordination is not settled on the authority of 1 Timothy or any other particular text, but rather on the basis of a different theological understanding of authority. In a new paradigm, authority might be understood as legitimate power only when it opens the way to inclusiveness and wholeness in the household of faith.

Master's tools. In chapter 1 I spoke of the devastating effects of living in the master's house of bondage by pointing to the alternative history of slavocracy from the perspective of Margaret Walker in *Jubilee*. But in order to see how oppression continues to exist even when we know about its devastation, we need to look at the tools used by the "master" to maintain the old house of authority.

One tool that continues to be used by elites of all color to control non-elites is *the assumption that the dominant group is right.* Whether this takes the extreme form of declaring that there is a divinely ordained hierarchy of human beings and nature that justifies the status quo or takes more subtle liberal forms of token inclusion, this tool of dominance is alive and well. This is underlined by Audrey Lorde in her essay "The Master's Tools Will Never Dismantle the Master's House," found in her wonderful collection of essays and speeches, *Sister Outsider*. Speaking at a New York University Institute for the Humanities Conference in 1979, she rejected the white feminist "tool" that had settled for bringing her to the conference as a token black lesbian feminist, rather than honoring a previous commitment to involve women of color in a dialogue on the role of "difference of race, sexuality, class, and age."[5] The master's tool that the white women scholars were using was the familiar tool of dominance; in this case, the racial and heterosexual dominance of the meeting's agenda.

Another tool that prevents the old house of authority from being challenged is that of *split consciousness*. Katie Cannon has described this dualistic view, perpetuated by the church, as an "idolatrous religion" that supports imperialism.[6] People are trained to separate different aspects of themselves and their lives so that they do not see any inconsistency in, for instance, being peace-loving Christians who support brutality at home and abroad. In her description of growing up in the South, Lillian Smith says:

> They who so gravely taught me to split my body from my mind and both from my "soul," taught me also to split my conscience from my acts and Christianity from southern tradition. . . . I learned it is possible to be a Christian and a white southerner simultaneously; to be a gentlewoman and an arrogant callous creature in the same moment; to pray at night and ride a Jim crow car the next morning and to feel comfortable in doing both.[7]

The tools are many and the struggles to face the terror of one's own fear in rejecting these tools are great.[8] But even in a most preliminary way we need to remember at least one additional tool, and that is *the necessity of control.* All forms of exercise of power as domination are legitimated with the appeal to "law and order" and the necessity for control in church and society. In the old divided plantation house, that control was achieved through the chain and whip and the adherence to countless regulations.[9] In our contemporary world, control continues to be achieved through a steady arms buildup—and a steady poverty buildup to pay for those arms. The constant appeal to order in theology as well as in politics masks the dis-order that results from holding so many persons in social, political, and economic bondage. In the challenge to this "established disorder," house revolutionaries who seek an authority of freedom are born.[10]

Cleansing the temple. One such house cleaner was Jesus. All four of the Gospels portray him as one who challenged the temple establishment of his time. John places the story of the entrance into Jerusalem, cleansing of the temple, and questions of authority at the beginning of his Gospel (John 2:13–22). The other three Gospels place the events at the beginning of the passion narrative (Matt. 21:1–17; Mark 11; Luke 19:28–20:8). In spite of the variations, however, it is clear that this particular confrontation was an important part of early Christian tradition. The different versions point ambiguously to future destruction of the temple, both in its identification with Jerusalem and Israel and with the death and resurrection of Jesus' own body (John 2:19; Mark 14:58; Matt. 26:61). They also point to fulfillment of the prophetic expectation that there will be a messianic purification of God's house (Mal. 3:1–12; Zech. 14:21; Jer. 7:11).[11] Like the jubilee, the purification of the temple was an eschatological sign of the restoration of God's righteousness.

It is likely that both the passover pilgrims and the priestly temple rulers who witnessed Jesus' action in overturning the tables of the money changers understood his symbolic action of house-cleaning as a prophetic protest against the temple banking system and the priestly system of taxation. The temple tax of one half shekel a year per adult male was levied on all the Jewish people to provide support for the priestly ruling class. This group, in turn, provided the religious sanctions for both religious and political oppression.[12] We can be fairly sure that both the priestly rulers and the people knew that Jesus was condemning not just the merchants but also their masters for profanation of God's house by using it for their own ends. This is why the Synoptic Gospels report that they sought to destroy him and began to question his authority (Luke 19:47–20:8).

When questioned about the source of his authority, Jesus refuses to answer except to identify his own prophetic actions with those of John the Baptist (Mark 11:28–30). The implication seems to be that Jesus' authority is from God and that those who do not recognize this bring judgment on themselves (Luke 19:41–44). As we saw in chapter 1, Jesus has authority (*exousia*) to forgive sins, heal, and preach good news. He refuses to use that authority for domination but, rather, uses it for the work of ushering in the new age. He also refuses to accept the religious split consciousness of his own day. He claims God's house as a "house of prayer for all nations" and welcomes foreigners and sinners alike into God's new household. Although John pictures Jesus using a whip of cords, the purpose of his actions was not to establish control but quite the opposite. He challenges the "disorder" of the religious establishment in the name of God's new order of freedom in community. The discussion of Jesus/Sophia in chapter 3 leads us to expect the conclusion of this story (2 Esdras 1:28–32). Then as now, the authorities seek to silence the troublemaker.

House Revolutionaries

Like Jesus in the temple, those who are "house revolutionaries" do not wish to destroy the house of authority. Quite the contrary, they wish to build it up again as a new house in which the authority of God's love and care for the outsiders is clearly seen. But in order to do this it is necessary to find ways of surviving in the master's house with those who still think according to the paradigm of domination. An important means of survival in the church is to know very clearly the way the old house of theological tradition was constructed.

Critical analysis. We have many resources for critical analysis, because modern theology, like philosophy, has long been occupied with "thinking about thinking." In the modern world, theologians have sought to maintain the enterprise of theological reflection when confronted by questions quite different from those for which they inherited the answers. One very detailed critique of classical theological method is that of Edward Farley. He also speaks of this theology as a "house of authority" and seeks to do what he calls "archaeology" of the old house. The purpose of his analysis is to expose its fragile pattern of verification, which can be toppled like a row of dominoes.[13] According to Farley, "classical theological thinking occurs, not in the mode of science but in the mode of authority."[14] Truth is decided with reference to that which has already been posited as God's revelation, rather than by an appeal to independent verification. The house itself has been made into an impregnable castle by always referring every question to some other room in the house of authority and by claiming that all the different parts of Christian doctrine must be true because they are based on God's sovereign will.[15]

Farley speaks of the house of authority as the "enemy" of truth and celebrates ways that it has already begun to collapse. His critical analysis is very helpful as we inquire about the paradigm of authority that is used in understanding Christian doctrine. I certainly agree that this paradigm is being challenged on many sides. Yet I am also aware that many religious structures are more authoritarian and reactionary than ever in order to compensate for the loss of legitimacy of that paradigm in modern society.[16] While valuing Farley's critique, I do not think that the house of authority as such is the enemy of truth. Rather, it is the master's house of patriarchal authority that needs replacement.

Tools for rebuilding. The house of authority needs rebuilding on a firm evangelical foundation like the "house upon the rock" (Matt. 7:24–27). We certainly need to begin with such critical analysis and then to add many other critiques, such as those of Beverly Harrison, Margaret Miles, Rosemary Ruether, Juan Luis Segundo, and Cornel West.[17] But as a "house revolutionary" I do not want to demolish the biblical and church tradition as a source of life, but to build a new house of authority using the "master's tools" in the service of the outsider. This new use of the tools includes not only critical analysis but also tools for rediscovering and rebuilding our theology while continuing to survive in the old house. Here Audrey Lorde is again helpful in proposing an alternative way of life and thought to that of dominance, "learning how to stand alone, unpopular and sometimes reviled, and how to make common cause with those others identified as outside the structures in order to define and seek a world in which we can all flourish."[18]

This, then, is the first tool to use as one tries to live as if the house of freedom were at hand in one's life: *Begin where you are*, and learn to make a stand for the freedom of your sisters and brothers and of yourself in that place (Gal. 5:1; Eph. 6:13–16). Christian vocation is a response to God's call in the place where you are called (1 Cor. 7:17–24). Do not wait for some distant ideal circumstance to live your life in a new way and to see things in a new way. Begin where you are to build up the new house from the foundation of your own experience and actions. Out of that ground it is possible to create a community of support who engage in what Delores Williams has called "lifeline politics."[19] As women of color are quick to show those of us who are white, it is possible to build solidarity in your community so that you continue the freedom journey even in the face of slavery and death. But this is a journey in the company of others and requires us to begin where we are and practice hospitality toward all who "seek a world in which we can all flourish."

Certainly feminist scholars have sought to begin where they are in their work of recovering, reinterpreting, and reconstructing the Christian tradition. Trained according to the prevailing academic paradigms, they have, nevertheless, made common cause with others who produce materials that reflect the questions and experiences of women. A good example of this is the selection of articles in the book I edited called *Feminist Interpretation of the Bible*. Here the scholars struggle with what Phyllis Trible has called "depatriarchalizing the Bible."[20] But they each do it in their own way, using the tools of their own field of scholarship and encouraging each person to approach the texts with what Katharine Sakenfeld describes as "a stance of radical suspicion" about the patriarchal bias of the writers as well as the interpreters.[21]

A second tool for rediscovery and rebuilding theological tradition is to *listen to the underside*. According to Luke 4:18–19, the gospel is good news for the poor and for those on the underside of society. If we want to understand that gospel and live it out, our interpretation cannot be based solely on our own critical analysis, experience, and vision. Our own particular theological paradigm needs to be stretched and expanded by the stories and insights both of those who themselves are victims of domination and of those who stand in solidarity with the victims and share their fate. This idea was not just invented by liberation and feminist theologians. Rather, they have begun to rediscover and to live out a continuing motif of the biblical story that stretches from the cries of the people in the house of bondage to the pleas of those outside the religious and political establishments of the ancient Near East. And this motif has continued to be alive and well in situations of adversity and struggle for life. In the early 1940s, for instance, Bonhoeffer wrote from prison:

> We have for once learnt to see the great events of world history from below, from the perspective of the outcast, the suspects, the maltreated, the powerless, the oppressed, the reviled—in short, from the perspective of those who suffer.[22]

What we learn from the underside becomes basic not only to the critique of the old house but also to the building up (*oikodomē*) of the new house of authority. Leonardo Boff, himself a victim of hierarchical thinking in the Roman Catholic Church, has made this very clear in his controversial book *Church: Charism and Power.*

> The sources of faith need to be reexamined, no longer with the eyes of those with power but with the eyes of all who have abandoned the perspective of power. In the past, ecclesiastical power read and reread the New Testament (almost only the epistles) for the first signs of thinking in terms of power, orthodoxy, tradition, preservation more than creation, moralizing more than prophetic proclamation. The cause of Christ, of the historical Jesus who was poor, weak, powerless, critical of the social and religious status quo of his time, was enshrined and spiritualized by the institution and so divested of its critical power.[23]

Listening to the underside puts us in touch with those who live by hope and not by nostalgia. Forming communities of struggle like the Base Ecclesial Communities described by Boff provides a hermeneutical key for interpretation.

Listening to the underside is a widespread form of feminist interpretation, for most of the women whose stories have survived in Bible and church tradition could be classed among the losers of their societies. The middle section of *Feminist Interpretation of the Bible*, "Feminists at Work," focuses respectively on the Syrophoenician woman, the image of Mother in Israel, Gomer as Hosea's unfaithful wife, and the struggles of battered women to make sense of biblical injunctions about obedience to husbands.[24] Elisabeth Fiorenza's outstanding work in the New Testament reconstructs social history from below, as a ministry to those women who find themselves victimized by teachings from the old house of authority. In *Bread Not Stone*, she writes:

A feminist critical hermeneutics of the household code texts has the aim, therefore, to become a "dangerous memory" that reclaims our foremothers' and foresisters' sufferings and struggles through the subversive power of the critically remembered past.[25]

A telling example of these sufferings and struggles is found in Phyllis Trible's *Texts of Terror*.[26] Elsa Tamez has also provided us with an interpretation of Hagar from the perspective of Latin American women struggling with slavery in their own lives; and there are, of course, countless other examples from all parts of the world.[27]

The last tool I want to suggest for rebuilding the house of authority is that of *working from the other end*. Theological thought is not just logical analysis of things as we think they are. It is full of imaginative uses of language and insight that help us picture what God is about in the work of mending creation and invite us to join in the process. Like Jesus' prophetic action in cleansing God's house, the metaphor "household of freedom" is an eschatological image. It seeks to spell out what living according to the paradigm of authority as partnership would look like in our everyday life, but it does this by pointing to God's intention of liberation and new creation. Even if we cannot see the alternative future for which we work, by beginning from the other end of God's promise we are able to live with a hope that is strong enough to transform the present.

This willingness to try living as if the future has already broken into our midst is what Jean Lambert calls the "F factor." In her view the *F* stands for both "feminist" and "future," as feminist theologians integrate their theological practice with their visions of a world of human wholeness. By beginning from their destination, these women are able to live now in relationships of respect and what Lambert calls "generosity toward divergent opinions," thus making a contribution to the style and to the content of biblical interpretation.[28]

A Place to Call Our Home

In the journey toward a new household of freedom, feminists are searching for what Doris Ellzey Blasoff has called "a new frontier,/A place to call our home."[29] In describing her own journey of faith, Nelle Morton says:

> I came to know home was not a place. Home is a movement, a quality of relationship, a state where people seek to be "their own," and increasingly responsible for the world.[30]

On our journey toward this new frontier we like Sophia/Christ
have found no dwelling place, "nowhere to lay [our] head." We
have only the authority of God's promised new household to guide
us on our way (Matt. 8:20). Because of this, some feminist interpreters use the tool of working from the other end in their search
for a place to call their home.

Searching for a place. These feminist and liberation views of
eschatology are similar to the proleptic eschatology of political
theologies or theologies of hope.[31] As we saw in chapter 1, the
future is understood as already—but not yet—present in its anticipations of God's new creation. The purpose in appealing to the
authority of the future is not to escape into otherworldly categories but to find the energy and vision for building a new house of
authority. In order to look at this eschatology as it is focused in
appeals to authority of the future, I will describe elements of this
theme in the work of Elisabeth Schüssler Fiorenza, Rosemary
Radford Ruether, and Alice Walker, before concluding with an
articulation of the authority of God's future in my own theology.

In her writings on feminist hermeneutic, Elisabeth Fiorenza has
argued that the authority to evoke consent should come from "the
experience of women (and all those oppressed) struggling for liberation from patriarchal oppression."[32] She disagrees with Ruether's method of correlating the prophetic-messianic tradition
with the feminist search for full human dignity for women, and
with my method of correlating the promise of mended creation
with the feminist search for human wholeness and partnership in
all creation. Rather than understanding both the biblical texts and
women's reality as possible loci of revelation, Fiorenza calls for a
single critical principle, based in the concrete life experience of
women and expressed in the political task of advocacy and liberating praxis. Thus she says:

> As I have already suggested in my contribution to *The Liberating
> Word*, feminist theology must first of all denounce all texts and tradi-
> tions that perpetrate and legitimate oppressive patriarchal structures
> and ideologies. We no longer should proclaim them as the "word of
> God" for contemporary communities and people if we do not want to
> turn God into a God of oppression.[33]

Fiorenza is no longer willing to play the authority game, submit-
ting feminist norms to "higher" biblical authority and androcen-
tric perceptions. Nevertheless, her appeal to the experience of
women turns out to be not just an authority of the present, or of
the past, but also very much an authority of the future. She says:

The common hermeneutical ground of past, present, and future is not "sacred history" or "sacred text" but commitment to the biblical vision of God's new creation.[34]

In opposing patriarchy as a root metaphor for hierarchical forms of social domination, Fiorenza presents *women-church* as a prototype for the discipleship community of equals and the hermeneutical center for feminist interpretation. Insofar as her historical reconstruction of women-church as "the movement of self-identified women and women-identified men in biblical religion" is based in the reconstruction of New Testament texts, it seems to me that it is still rooted in biblical eschatology.[35] For the early egalitarian Christian community was the eschatological community gathered in response to the power of the resurrection to live out the teachings of Jesus as anticipations of the Coming One.

Rosemary Ruether has responded to Elisabeth Fiorenza's critique of her correlation between the feminist critical principle of promoting the full humanity of women and the biblical critical principle of the prophetic-messianic tradition. Ruether contends that this tradition, drawn from the prophetic stream of the Old Testament and from the liberating motifs of the Gospels, is not a set of texts or a canon within a canon. It is

a critical perspective and process through which the biblical tradition constantly reevaluates, in new contexts, what is truly the liberating Word of God, over against both the sinful deformations of contemporary society and also the limitations of past biblical traditions, which saw in part and understood in part.[36]

Like all tradition, this particular tradition undergoes many revisions in the biblical materials and continues to need revision and interpretation in new contexts.

Ruether is also appealing to the future as well as the past as her basis of authority. Although the prophets had little concern for the oppression of women, they nevertheless exercised the same prophetic imagination in the face of injustice that continued to inform Jesus' ministry to the poor and to women, as a sign of God's welcome of all those outcasts of society into God's reign. In searching out an eschatology that is no longer used in a dualistic way as an excuse for the domination of women's bodies and of the earth, Ruether turns to the jubilee and Sabbath traditions in their combination of linear and cyclical patterns. As I indicated in chapter 1, this tradition in Leviticus 25:8–12 calls for a continual return to the "basic elements that make up life as God intended it." Although rejecting any form of eschatology that is "endless flight into an unrealized future," Ruether looks to images of the wholeness of creation as both a recalling and an anticipation of the ingredients of a just and livable society.[37] She continues to search for materials that can provide "womanguides" from the marginalized communities at the edges of Judaism and Christianity in order to keep this promised future of God open for women.[38]

Alice Walker is a black "womanist" writer and not a theologian. Yet, as Carter Heyward has said, "it is hard to imagine a more compelling example of feminist consciousness, so critical to feminist theology, than Alice Walker's sensitivity to the dynamics of women's lives in *The Color Purple*."[39] Not only does Walker make it clear that the white male patriarchal God is an idol, she also draws her readers into looking for alternative ways of relating to God as one who cares about people. In chapter 3 I described the way Celie's friend Shug instructs her about false images, saying, "When I found out I thought God was white, and a man, I lost interest." She goes on later to help Celie see that giving up the white man's God does not mean that we lose God, but rather that we have the possibility of finding God as one who loves "everything you love" (including the color purple), and wants to be loved in return![40]

Walker knows about the tools for rebuilding. She begins where she is and invites her readers to listen to the underside. And out of the context of black struggles for freedom against oppression, she speaks clearly of the suffering hope that keeps her people on their seemingly hopeless journey in a racist society. On a 1984 radio broadcast she said:

> *The Colo₁ rurple* is a message to my ancestors that I understand their traditions and ways are quite valuable and adequate in deciding many issues in life. I have learned from them that you can be oppressed, depressed, repressed, and suppressed and fight your way through it.[41]

The source of that hope for Walker is in solidarity with her community. She writes in *In Search of Our Mothers' Gardens* that what a black southern writer inherits "as a natural right is a sense of community."[42] And out of that community comes the belief that people can change, that there is an authority not only of the ancestors but also of their hope. Change is what is going on in the life of Mr., Celie's husband in *The Color Purple*. He is transformed from a cruel, sexist man, to whom Celie will not remain married, into a man with integrity and insight. Still, he is someone with whom Celie continues to share community and hope.

> I believe in change: change personal, and change in society. I have experienced a revolution (unfinished, without question, but one

whose new order is everywhere on view) in the South. And I grew up—until I refused to go—in the Methodist church, which taught me that Paul *will* sometimes change on the way to Damascus, and that Moses—that beloved old man—went through so many changes he made God mad.[43]

Mending creation. None of these feminist writers would necessarily say that authority of the future is a key element in their feminist theory. In fact, their respective concerns for biblical historical reconstruction, theological reinterpretation, and Afro-American culture seem to point toward the search for a usable past. Yet out of the articulation of women's struggles comes a longing for freedom that points to an anticipation of a society that has moved beyond oppression. In my own theology I have tried to image this world beyond oppression as a mended creation in which human beings, nature, and all creation are set free from their groaning and are at home with one another.[44] This image also functions as a hermeneutical key for interpretation of scripture and tradition. With Ruether, I see a correlation between the feminist critical principle of promoting the full humanity of women— and restoring the partnership of human beings with themselves, one another, God, and nature—and the biblical critical principle of promoting the mending of God's world house.

I first heard this simple expression of eschatological hope from Krister Stendahl, who said that theology is worrying about what God is worrying about when God gets up in the morning: the mending of creation.[45] The image itself appeals to me because it evokes both the biblical message of promise on the way to fulfill-ment and a feminine image of God as the one who cares enough for creation to mend it. Although the evidence that God intends women to be included in the mending of creation is seldom self-evident in the patriarchal context of the biblical texts, they never-theless hold out a vision of liberation that continues to have authority in my life and faith.

For me, the mending of creation begins with the jubilee image of liberation for the oppressed (Luke 4:16–19). Women are the "oppressed of the oppressed" in every land; there will be no new household of freedom if these women have no part in it. Articulation of the pain of oppression is a crucial source of understanding in liberation and feminist theologies, and there is a great deal of wisdom that is available and waiting to be heard in their groans. As a white member of an affluent oppressor nation, I can only live out of the authority of this future when I am willing to look deeply at my own pain and fear and to risk "betraying the betrayers" of the victims of racism, sexism, and capitalism.[46]

My urgent agenda for participating in this future of the oppressed is to find continuing ways to stand in solidarity with those who are able to live out of the authority of that future because they have already lived through the worst that could be done to them. As Katie Cannon has pointed out, it is women like Fannie Lou Hamer who portray for us what redemption means as it is lived among us.[47] In 1963 this Mississippi sharecropper responded to the call for voter registration and risked her life to register. She was arrested and beaten so viciously that she was permanently debilitated, but she never gave up her struggle for freedom. Fannie Lou Hamer had been to the bottom and she knew that she was willing to die for the freedom of her people. No one could touch her any more. She only knew the authority of future's freedom and the journey with others toward a new frontier, a place to call her home.

This new house of authority belongs to God, the housekeeper of all creation. Against the old house of patriarchal bondage, God stands as the One who suffers the cost of sin and domination and rebuilds creation itself through the work of Jesus Christ. And God has invited us to join as partners in the work of cleansing the temple and rebuilding creation. Because of the memory of God's future, we continue to hope and to plan according to the utopian vision of the new household of freedom. Thus we can affirm, with Dorothee Soelle:

> Human work is aimed at re-creating the world and transforming it into what Ernst Bloch in his *Principle of Hope* calls "a home that no one has entered." . . . It is through our most humane activities, in work and in love, that we become co-creators of the new earth, the place we may finally call home.[48]

5

Household, Power, and Glory

People everywhere experience the social and spiritual manifestations of the paradigm of authority as domination and its metaphors of bondage. In most circumstances they also accept this view of reality and remain trapped in the power structures of our world, described in the New Testament translations as "principalities and powers." But, as we saw in chapter 4, there are people who become aware of the possibility of a change in that reality and begin to make a stand against the powers. Those who are Christians draw their courage and strength from the memory of the future: the memory of a Messiah or Savior who stood with the people against the powers, was crucified by these powers, yet continues to live victorious in their midst. The presence of Christ among the people establishes signs of a new political reality in which persons have the possibility of life together in freedom and community.[1]

The expectation of a messianic fulfillment of God's promises for a household of freedom arises in concrete circumstances where people are struggling against the powers of sexist, classist, and racist oppression. Here the authority of the future takes root and eschatology provides a dimension of liberation in the midst of struggle and resistance. The articulation of "hope against hope" in situations of "no hope" becomes a transcendent dimension of life in the midst of death (Rom. 4:18).

One example of this articulation is the development of Minjung theology in the midst of the Korean struggle for human rights. As Kim Yong-Bock writes in his article "Messiah and Minjung," the "messianic aspirations of the people arise out of the historical confrontation between the people and the powers."[2] In the context of oppression, a small part of the Korean Christian church has become a confessional church, which supports those who are willing to be fired, harassed, jailed, tortured, and killed in order to become advocates of unity, democracy, and freedom in Korea.

On a visit to South Korea in 1983 I was privileged to share the stories and reflections of a host of such witnesses. In Kwangju on the third anniversary of the Kwangju massacre, I spoke with YWCA women in their temporary headquarters. During the massacre the student demonstrators had sought refuge in the YWCA building, only to be attacked by the military with such firepower that the building became unsafe for further use. My hostess, the retired General Secretary, Cho a La, had been jailed along with many others. Her crime was that at seventy years of age she still insisted on joining other leaders in trying to negotiate with the government to prevent the shooting and work for peace.

Now finally out of jail, she invited me to share with other Christians who were preparing to carry out a memorial worship service and illegal gathering at the church. We went for a simple meal beforehand, around the corner. My friends laughed and talked about plans for a new building. They were silent and worried as well. Cho a La said that the only thing she had with her was her medicine. If she were arrested she could not survive without it. In this discussion of preparations for arrest, there was no great show of courage, only a community of ordinary women gathered as a small household of freedom to resist the idolatrous pretensions of state power.

People and the Powers

Theologians from Asia, Africa, and Latin America alike remind us that our economic and political rulers are included among those who offer the false hopes of political messianism.[3] In political messianism the language of war, conquest, and development is couched in the offer of national power, pride, and prosperity. This in turn conceals the reality of victimization and despair among the exploited, poor, starving, and dying peoples whose lives sustain that rhetoric. Among those exploited by political messianism are the women who are the poor of the poor, the minjung of the minjung, the oppressed of the oppressed. One thinks for instance of those killed, raped, and brutally separated from husbands and children in war; of those driven to prostitution in order to feed their families or reduced to blindness at the age of thirty from bending over a microscope to produce microchips for our computers.

Messianic politics. All too frequently the response of the Christian churches to this situation of idolatry, in which nations have become as gods, is another form of false messianism, a spiritualized message of salvation which offers salvation of the soul while ignoring the cries of God's people and God's intention of justice. Feminist and liberation theologians resist this spiritualized message by proclaiming a form of expectant hope that is rooted in political and social reality. Kim Yong-Bock calls this "messianic politics" because it retains the dimension of divine transcendence, through identification with the work of the Messiah, but is rooted in the experience of the minjung: the politically oppressed, economically exploited, socially marginalized, and culturally despised and ignored people of Korea.[4]

This form of eschatology locates the mandate for social justice not in some secular ideology but in the resurrection itself. Thus Rubem Alves says that the language of resurrection portrays Jesus as "not a *fact*, simply, but rather the *factor* of history, the power of freedom that creates the facts of liberation."[5] And a feminist theologian like Rosemary Ruether writes:

> The primary vision of salvation in the Bible is that of an alternative future, a new society of peace and justice that will arise when the present systems of injustice have been overthrown.[6]

The story of the suffering Messiah provides a paradigm for understanding the collective messianic role of the oppressed in struggling for freedom. Messianic politics is understood as a political process in which, as Yong-Bock says, the minjung join the Messiah in realizing the messianic role, while political (ruling class) messianism attempts to use and sacrifice the minjung to its own false messianic claims.[7]

This identification of the poor and marginalized with the history of the Messiah is not new. It appears to be the intent of the parable of the last judgment in Matthew 25:31–46. According to Matthew, Jesus is not just providing us with a description of church history or world history; rather, he is telling his own history of identification of the poor and outcast so that, together with the Messiah, all who hunger or thirst, all who are naked, sick, or in prison, become the real presence of God's mending work.[8] In solidarity with the least of Jesus' brothers and sisters we find a social biography of struggle that continues Jesus' own story. This is not because the oppressed are more righteous than the oppressors. It is because serving the cause of Jesus and welcoming the outcasts into society is sign of God's presence in our midst, a sign of God's household, power, and glory. As Krister Stendahl has put it, praying for the coming of God's kingdom is praying for a redeemed, healed, mended world household.

> Wherever, whenever, however the kingdom manifests itself, it is welcome: in a healed body, in a restored mind, in a more just society, in a human heart that finds the power to forgive, in the faith and trust of a Canaanite mother, in the death and resurrection of the Messiah, in a new heaven and a new earth where justice dwells.[9]

Those who are considered "the sinners and tax collectors," the rejects of any society, are also the center of the story of salvation because it is they who can tell when God's will is being done (Mark 2:13-17). They are the ones who must be about remaking society if it is going to be a significant "re-making."[10] For the victims of society know if justice is being done and if creation is being mended. With Zacchaeus, their joy is great when they find themselves included in the plans of God's Messiah. Luke's story portrays Zacchaeus as a rich tax collector for imperial Rome, an outcast in his own society who longed for acceptance (Luke 19:1-10). Jesus' invitation to come down from the tree and provide hospitality offers him a chance to change. In identifying with messianic politics, everyone has the opportunity to repent and to join the struggle to include all persons in God's household of freedom (Matt. 5:25). This is not just past history, it is the present story of Jesus, a story that can become our story. Thus Gustavo Gutiérrez says:

> When you place your hope in the Lord and sink your roots into the concrete power of the poor in history, you are not living in nostalgia. You are living in a present moment, whose direction is forward.[11]

Building coalitions. When this story becomes our story, we find ourselves in a movement with many other very different kinds of persons, yet we come to share the same new household. Bernice Johnson Reagon makes the difficulty of such coalitions for change explicit.

> You don't go into a coalition because you just *like* it. The only reason you would consider trying to team up with someone who could possibly kill you is because that's the only way you can figure you can stay alive.[12]

I often find myself caught in such coalition problems because, like many other white middle-class women, I am "status inconsistent." I belong to a very privileged group identified by race, nationality, education, and occupation with oppressor groups who just might kill (and do kill) uppity black women like Bernice Johnson Reagon, a leading singer in the Sweet Honey in the Rock ensemble. Yet as a woman I am also a member of a dominated group and in need of coalitions with persons in other dominated groups as I seek to participate in messianic politics. Any woman or man of color has good reason to distrust me, and I have good reason to distrust men of every color. Yet work together we must.

One experience I had of this difficult and risky coalition building was at an international conference of the Ecumenical Association of Third World Theologians, held in Geneva in 1983.[13] After meeting by themselves for a period of years, the third-world theologians invited liberation and feminist theologians from the first world to participate in a dialogue. This was a very exciting time for me because the people present all shared what could be called a commitment to messianic politics. We made use of similar theological methods, beginning with the stories of struggle in our own context to understand God's action of liberation in that place and to participate in that mission. But there was a great deal of suspicion directed at those of us who came from oppressor races and nations, and I felt a great deal of suspicion toward delegations from third-world countries that were largely male.

I discovered, however, that there was a point at which we all could come together to hear one another into speech and action, and that was at the *point of pain*. The theology that we did together became liberation theology as we discovered our own marginalization or cross as a result of our commitment to oppressed people. In suffering there is not only solidarity with the people, there is also empowerment to share together in Christ's messianic sufferings (Mark 10:35). Messianic politics includes the suffering that comes with opposing the principalities and powers. At the hands of these powers, the "kingdom of heaven suffers violence," and those who work to keep it from being snatched away may find that their journey is not without risk. Speaking about this difficult saying from Matthew 11:12, Marta Benavides has described her ministry in the midst of the violence of El Salvador in the following way:

> You have to have *faith* in God just to be able to sleep at all. You have to *believe* in the people just to get out of bed; believe that you can do what needs to be done. You have to "baptize" yourself each day to get the will to conspire for peace.[14]

Against the Powers

The conviction of messianic politics is that there is power among the people to stand against the powers, but that this is clearly not without cost. The term "powers" in messianic politics refers to the language of power that, according to Walter Wink, pervades the whole New Testament, for "no New Testament book is without the language of power."[15] The familiar translation of *archai* and *exousiai* as "principalities and powers" is the focal point of much research about the powers, but the New Testament has many other paired words and strings of words for: power, authority, rulers, kings, angels, chief priests, name, wisdom, and commission. In teaching with authority and using his healing power to exorcize demonic powers, Jesus confronted both seen and unseen powers and paid the cost of this confrontation. His life, death, and resurrection were all signs that the rule of God was coming in power and glory to confront the old structures of death and domination. By his actions Jesus empowers others to faith, new life, and partnership in God's new reality.

Naming the powers. The terms for power in the New Testament are fluid and imprecise, and the translations of the terms magnify that imprecision. But according to Wink we can discern a pattern in the use of the words, as, for instance, with the two words often translated "authority" and "power."

> *Exousia* denotes the legitimations and sanctions by which power is maintained; it generally tends to be abstract. *Dynamis* overlaps with *exousia* in the area of sanctions; it refers to power or force by which rule is maintained.[16]

The powers are understood as both good and evil, heavenly and earthly, divine and human, spiritual and political, invisible and structural. Every outward social or political structure is understood as also having an inward spiritual aspect, but in Wink's view they are generally encountered in some outward form. For instance, "principalities and powers" indicates human agents and institutions in the two places it appears in the Gospels, Luke 12:11 and 20:20. The other eight occurrences, more complex in reference but with both heavenly and earthly meanings, are found in the Pauline and post-Pauline epistles.[17]

Ephesians 6:10–20 gives us a very good example of the piling up of power words to demonstrate what Christians are up against as they seek to live out a life of faith. Using the image of the armor of God that is strong enough to protect God's people, the author declares:

> For we are not contending against flesh and blood, but against the principalities, against the powers, against the world rulers of this present evil age, against the spiritual hosts of wickedness in the heav-

enly places. Therefore take the whole armor of God, that you may be able to withstand in the evil day, and having done all, to stand (Eph. 6:12–13).

The imagery of powers here is so poetic that it is hard to say exactly what is meant. But, according to Marcus Barth, it probably means "those institutions and structures by which earthly matters and invisible realms are administered and without which no human life is possible."[18] In modern times we might call these the social, political, economic, cultural, and biological structures that guide world history, as long as we remember that they are not "just political structures" but also contain spiritual power as well.[19] Under the influence of the power of evil, they oppose the power of good and those who seek to live under that power. Just as God's power fills both heaven and earth, these powers are able to operate in all spheres of creation and therefore are called "spiritual hosts of wickedness in heavenly places."

Those who want to withstand these powers are assured of the power and victory of God's love, but in the meanwhile their task is to *make a stand* against unjust and oppressive powers. Their splendid armor is designed by God to help make that stand in the real world. Like the little nation of Nicaragua today as it faces the U.S. military giant, the little churches of Asia Minor had no hope except God and those who shared their longing for a new household of freedom. This "ragtag band" on its way to the Promised Land was equipped with the Spirit of God, not by its own doing but by the One who chose to equip them with the gospel of peace even when they were under attack.

It seems here that this passage goes against everything that I have been saying about the possibility of alternative paradigms for power and authority. The author appears to encourage the struggling Ephesian community to emulate the patriarchal oppressor and take over the Roman armor, the master's tools. In Ephesians 6:20, however, we discover that the social location of the speaker is pictured as a jail cell, not a battlefield. Paul is described as an "ambassador in chains." As a prisoner for Christ he is able to look out at the armor of his Roman guard and put it to a different use, renaming the pieces of the armor as the Messianic gifts of peace, righteousness, truth, faithfulness, and "equity for the meek of the earth" (Isa. 11:2–7).

Even so, this military metaphor is drawn straight from the paradigm of authority as domination, and it can be a dangerous masculine image of courage in our world, so full of violence. How one works for peace and opposes the powers depends on the place one is standing. The biblical message, like all messages, is "situation variable" and can mean different things in different places. This Ephesian text about armor can be a dangerous excuse for triumphalism and military glorification when heard by people who are powerful, or a dangerous cop-out for disembodied spirituality when used as an otherworldly message for the comfortable. On the other hand, those who are struggling for life against death, struggling like the early Christian communities, may very well find that these words about the power of God's love can keep them going when all else fails.

Transforming the powers. This is why there can be no one description of powers or authorities and of how they may be transformed by God.[20] Transforming the powers when one is in a subordinate power location may mean actions of confrontation, while it may mean abdication or reconciliation when one is part of the more powerful group. *Situation variability* is an important first clue for dealing with authority and power in such a way that one moves toward authorizing and empowerment, in spite of all the ambiguities of any social situation.

For instance, the amount of ability one has to accomplish a particular end often determines what might be a possible strategy. I have often said, "I only fight with friends," thinking that this is because I am too sensitive, too afraid to do otherwise, or I really do not like to hurt people and so only enjoy arguing or competing when there is mutual trust and no intent to hurt. But according to critical analysis of power relationships, I also see that one only fights in an old-fashioned toe-to-toe combat in a situation of equality. Otherwise one seeks other ways to settle with the one who already has most of the power. This is why guerrilla warfare is so popular. It also helps to explain why women often have to resort to manipulation to accomplish their goals.

A similar analysis of power relationships is needed to understand why women who enter the professional ministry have so much difficulty dealing with power and authority. When they are called to their first parish and decide to exercise authority as partnership, they often find that this does not work. The new pastor does not realize that power is situation variable. She cannot decide to share power and work in a process of empowerment until her authority has been recognized as legitimate by the congregation. She has the legitimacy of employment and ordination, but the congregation may not perceive her as legitimate because she does not fit the accustomed father role. Through spending time in pastoral caring and in clarifying the job description, in decision making, and in communication, she may overcome initial sexist attitudes and be able to come to a point of self-empowerment and sharing of power with others. The strategies of messianic politics vary according to the situation and the power positions involved.

A second clue for making a stand against the powers is to remember that *the weak do have power*. The weak can exercise their power in destructive or constructive ways, just like the strong. They have the same ability to accomplish desired goals, even though the weak may have to work in different styles because of the power differential. According to Hannah Arendt, power is always a "power potential" and is always changeable.[21] The people are the source of power because they are the ones who cooperate with the powers. It is both the obedience and the productivity of those who are weak that contributes to the power of the strong.

Power comes into existence between persons because they respond through habit to the authority, reward systems, expertise, skills, and language used by those in control.[22] But people can also question this process of obedience. For instance, Elizabeth Janeway has pointed out that two such powers are "disbelief" and "coming together."[23] Disbelief is a way of delegitimatizing the power exerted by authorities through their language and paradigms of thought and action. Because authority only works when the relationship of assent is accepted by the less powerful parties, disbelief becomes a powerful tool for standing against the powers. And coming together provides the solidarity, support systems, and friendships that make it possible for the weak to retain their vision of an alternative society and world.[24]

A final clue for those who wish to stand against the powers in order to create a new household of freedom is to *avoid dualism*. In our brief analysis of the powers, as well as of messianic politics, we have seen that those who allow a dualistic view of either structural or spiritual powers, either political or individual salvation, do not have an adequate analysis of the strength of the powers of domination in their lives. The armor of God's love is all the more necessary because the powers are not just flesh and blood; they are also corporate spirits of domination that rule our minds and spirits. As we saw, messianic politics combines both the political and the transcendent dimensions of the struggle of the people against the powers and refuses to let the struggle be understood either as purely secular or purely spiritual.

In the same way, Wink has helped us understand that the powers always include both the spiritual and the material aspects of the hierarchies of domination and evil. An example Wink has given comes from a conversation he had with a woman he met on a trip to Latin America. The woman had been brutally tortured, and she was trying to understand how people could be so evil and utterly inhuman. As Wink put it, "Idolatry to the Powers captures people. People give themselves over to the idols, in the name of which an evil is good if it serves that idol."[25] For instance, the idol of national security justifies military buildup, denial of human rights, and murder because anything opposed to such an idol is evil. Against such idols of death, Christians and all women and men of courage must choose life and refuse to accept domination of the death-dealing powers (Deut. 30:19).[26]

Household of God

The presence of Christ among those who confront the authorities of domination creates the possibility of a new household of freedom where persons are able to relate to one another in an authority of partnership. But households of freedom are not in themselves "the power and the glory." Rather, they are signs of the power of God's kingdom at work in our midst, through the praxis of messianic politics. They are signs that the new household of God is not just a spiritual abstraction, separated from the suffering of the world, but rather a present reality in the discipleship of women and men who break bread together, and with the poor and wretched of the earth

Power and glory. The struggle of people against the powers is well illustrated in Graham Greene's 1940 novel about religious persecution in Mexico, *The Power and the Glory.*[27] In it the martyr-priest becomes one of the persecuted people because of his seeming inability to escape. Green contrasts this one messianic figure, who is a "whiskey priest," with another who is a military lieutenant bent on saving the people even if he has to kill hostages in every village. In this novel, the power and the glory struggle to be born out of the lives of marginal people who are the nobodies of the church and of the world. But the dualistic view of religion among the people allows the priest to think of himself as a sinner and wino and yet a man of God who holds the means of salvation through the wine and bread. In the same way the lieutenant sees himself as a savior of his people and yet a man of war who holds the means of life and death through violence.

A glimpse of power and glory is there in this crucifixion drama, but one is left with a fatalistic form of patriarchal religion that means suffering for the people, and a revolution that means only more suffering. The alternative of messianic politics would claim that a stand against the powers can be made as part of one's religious commitment and not against it. In fact, such a stand for justice and shalom is a sign of God's power at work creating households of freedom; a sign of "the kingdom and the power and the glory."

The metaphor used in the New Testament for the presence of God's gracious power is that of the kingdom or reign of God. Although drawn from the social reality of the biblical world, the language of kingdom was not intended to show God's reign as like that of Caesar. Rather, the use of the term in the parables and parabolic actions of Jesus was iconoclastic. Jesus' actions reveal that he had turned the word "kingdom" on its head so that those at the bottom of the old house of authority became first in the kingdom of God (Mark 10:14; Matt. 19:30). Thus, Rosemary Ruether says, "in the iconoclastic messianic vision, it is the women of the despised and the outcast peoples who are seen as the bottom of the present hierarchy and hence, in a special way, the last who shall be first in the kingdom."[28] In the same way the "fatherhood of God" is proclaimed against the fathers of the patriarchal household, and those seeking the kingdom are identified as children of God: brothers, sisters, friends of one another (Matt. 18:2–4).[29]

Kingdom as household. Scholars have a great deal of difficulty translating the kingdom metaphor, but most hold that it is intended not to convey a spatial image of place but rather a relational image of obedience. God's reign occurs in all places, in heaven as on earth, wherever people do God's will of mending the creation. It seems to me that one way of making it clear that the gospel confronts the old image of kingdom as domination and exclusion and replaces it with a new image of kingdom as love and community is to use an alternative metaphor, that of the household. As we have seen, the metaphor often used in the parables to convey the message of God's hospitality is the household, or *oikos*. For instance, the parable of the leaven compares the household (kingdom) of God to "leaven which a woman took and hid in three measures of meal, till it was all leavened" (Luke 13:20–21). If we were to pray "For thine is the *household* and the power and the glory," this might convey to us that God's power and glory are to be seen not in domination but in the daily housekeeping of God's world. God's power works like leaven, in humble circumstances, but in a way that transforms both personal and social relationships.[30]

Domestic images for the kingdom abound in the New Testament. A favorite is that of table fellowship. In his *New Testament Hospitality*, John Koenig says that "the images of God's kingdom

that predominate overwhelmingly in Jesus' teaching are those associated with the production of food and drink or home-like refuge for God's creatures."[31] Such festive household meals are
"jubilee celebrations" to which outsiders, the poor, the sick and
disabled, tax collectors, sinners, and prostitutes are all welcome
(Luke 14:15–24).

In Mark 3:24–25, the kingdom (*basileia*) and household (*oikia*)
are used interchangeably, as well they might be, for a kingdom is
the "house" of a ruler.

> If a kingdom is divided against itself, that kingdom cannot stand.
> And if a house is divided against itself, that house will not be able to
> stand.

The Matthew 12:25 version of this parable also uses *polis* (city)
interchangeably with *basileia* and *oikia*. As a metaphor of God's
reign, the household can transcend the divisions between "oikos"
and "polis," between public and private sectors, and claim the
whole as the arena of God's powerful love. This is consistent with
the "basileia vision of Jesus," which was one of "inclusive wholeness."[32]

In addition to word and metaphor association between household and kingdom, we find household imagery is associated with
the parousia in different parts of the New Testament. One thinks
not only of the John 14:2 passage about the heavenly temple or
dwelling place but also of texts that compare the house or body to
the heavenly body (2 Cor. 5:1–10; 2 Peter 1:13). The new community built up as a household by Christ is also one that can withstand the "powers of death" (Matt. 16:18).[33] Here the household is
called the church (*ekklēsia*). As I already noted in chapter 2, the
use of the metaphor of household gradually disappears in its eschatological form and becomes identified with the church in later
New Testament traditions.

This raises both a problem and a possibility for using the term
"household of God" for the kingdom of God. It confuses people
who have come to associate the term with the household-of-God
language in 1 Peter. There the writer speaks of building up the
church community as a "home for the homeless," as well as of the
judgment that begins in the church as the household of God (1
Peter 2:4–10; 4:17).[34] In the New Testament there is always the
understanding that the household can be the gathered community, but it also can be the eschatological reality of a new heaven
and new earth.

The Christian people are not the only ones who belong in God's
household, as we have seen from Matthew 25. It is important to

broaden our vision of what household might mean, not only beyond the old Roman household of domination of women, slaves,
and children in the private sector, but also beyond Israel and the
church. The church as a household of faith is called to be a sign of
God's power at work among all the nations of the *oikoumenē*, but
there are other signs that point toward God's mended world
house.[35]

People who are victims of the powers are also welcomed by
Christ into his story as participants in building new households of
freedom. Surely they too must become for us a messianic sign, a
sacrament of the poor. Along with the sacrament of the household
meal, the sacrament of the poor speaks of God's welcome as
housekeeper and Christ's presence as servant. This presence is
hidden among the "little ones," who refuse to give up hope as they
stand against the powers. As Adrienne Rich has put it in her poem
"Natural Resources":

> My heart is moved by all I cannot save: so much has been destroyed
> I have to cast my lot with those who age after age, perversely,
> with no extraordinary power, reconstitute the world.[36]

6

Good Housekeeping

A discussion of good housekeeping seems appropriate for a book that develops "household of freedom" as a metaphor for authority in partnership. Certainly there has been a great deal of talk of "bad housekeeping" in the household of bondage. Yet the experience of the feminist touch, turning the questions of feminists into questions of authority, has warned us that the patriarchal paradigm of authority as domination controls the minds, hearts, and institutions of church and society. A great deal of housecleaning is in order if the church is to live out its calling as an eschatological sign and instrument sign of God's household.[1]

Questions multiply from every direction as we try to picture ourselves in new relationships of authority. How can our families, congregations, trade unions, offices, political parties, schools, advocacy groups, and so on look a little more like households of freedom? How would we recognize a household of freedom if we were lucky enough to stumble across its threshold? How would we care for such a household, and work to build it up as a sign of God's good housekeeping intentions for the world? What are the implications of a new paradigm of authority for reinterpreting biblical theology, ecclesiology, or ethics of family life?

It is a mistake to assume that the last chapter of a book on theology should end with "the answers." In the first place, there are no easy answers to such difficult questions. Households happen where mutual love, care, and trust happen. They are not mass produced; there are no prefab households! There is only the possibility of checking out some of the clues about paradigms of authority, asking if they make sense in the lives of those who are struggling to create partnership in a world of division. In the second place, this is not the style of feminist/liberation theologies. They do not begin with theory and move to practice. Rather, they begin with the communities of faith and struggle who are acting in new ways, and then ask how this experience leads to new questions and ways of thinking.

Although I do not have any easy answers and examples, what I have been saying is founded in my experience and in the experience of many other women and men who are critical of the hierarchical structures in our churches and societies today. In fact, I have spent thirty-five years trying to find out how to subvert the church into being the church! Working in the East Harlem Protestant Parish, I helped design missionary structures of the congregation, and from the 1960s until now I have never stopped trying to find a way to make the church into an "open circle" of those gathered in Christ's name for service to and with others.

For a while I thought I had found the heart of the problem: the "clergy line." It seemed that every restructuring would always end in a pyramid if some had higher status than others in our congregations. But I have gradually come to see that the issue of authority underlies even that issue, because the meaning and function of ordination is determined by how we picture the authority conferred in ordination. At present I am serving on the Faith and Order commissions of the National Council of Churches and the World Council of Churches, studying "The Unity of the Church and the Renewal of Human Community."[2] This study is trying to find out how the experience of churches struggling for human renewal leads to new ecclesial self-understanding and new perspectives on unity. A still unresolved problem of the study is again what theological paradigm of authority will decide the methods and questions of the study.[3]

This book began with several years of action and reflection with sisters and brothers engaged in struggle against the patriarchal paradigm of domination and its legitimization of oppression. In it I am reflecting on what people are already doing to create new households of freedom. Their stories and accumulated wisdom make it possible to ask if indeed a new paradigm of authority would make better sense of their experiences. In 1981 I published *Growth in Partnership* in order to explore how relationships of mutuality are nurtured.[4] But examples of change do not create change without a shift in perspective. As we saw in chapter 2, a change in paradigm happens for persons, disciplines, and entire societies as accumulated experiences of cognitive dissonance lead to conversion. People see and act differently when the old paradigm of domination no longer makes sense and they are somehow forced to turn around and welcome the messengers of God's household!

In this final chapter the hints about good housekeeping and bad housekeeping are not intended as answers to our questions but as clues that might help us on our continuing journey. After a brief analysis of how authority of domination functions through forms of paternalism and autonomy, I will look for clues to building up households of freedom that may be found in partnering relationships. Finally, the signs of God's own partnership with the "least of our brothers and sisters" become a continuing clue for our journey home. On this journey only the Spirit grants Good Housekeeping seals of approval, but our own limited perspective can give us a few hints about how to "keep on keeping on" toward a household of freedom.

Paternalism and Autonomy

When we turn to ask how this understanding of authority *in* community is expressed in Christian churches today, we find that the more usual model is that of authority *over* community. Without much effort we can discover that churches still carry with them a great deal of the baggage of the patriarchal understanding of authority that was shaped in the social world of the ancient Near East, rather than the partnering paradigm exhibited in Jesus' own critique of hierarchy and solidarity with the outcasts of society.

Relational bond. In his book *Authority*, Richard Sennett helps us to understand some of the social and psychological dynamics of relationships of authority as they have evolved in the history of the church. He describes authority as a relational bond that leads persons to give assent without coercion or persuasion because they find needed security in the real or imagined strength of others.[5] His analysis helps us to see how patriarchy changes and yet continues in our churches and society in illegitimate forms of paternalism and autonomy that undercut more mature relationships of partnership. His analysis is also important for family relationships, where authority of domination continues to legitimize many kinds of psychological and physical brutality.[6]

According to Sennett's sociohistorical description, "patriarchy" refers to social relationships in which people are consciously related by blood ties to elder males, who claim obedience through these ties. Although this tradition of authority was called into question by Jesus' teaching about God's household and by some of the models of early church life, it was reinforced by the culture of the Roman empire as well as the theological traditions that portrayed God as the ruling patriarch.

In Western medieval society the evolving paradigm of authority was patrimonial. Control rested in the hands of the eldest males because property was handed down from one generation to the next through this male line. But the advent of modern industrial society has resulted in the gradual erosion of patrimony so that we now live in a Western world where two patterns of patriarchal authority predominate, paternalism and autonomy.[7]

Sennett describes *paternalism* as a form of male domination without a contract. Males still use the language of patriarchy, but they seldom have the property or power to provide security to those who consent to their control. He calls paternalism an authority of false love which claims to offer nurture and care but leads to dependence.

The other illegitimate form of modern patriarchal authority is *autonomy*. Male dominance in society is perpetuated by those who have rebelled against paternalism and sought to free the individual from dependence on anyone else. Such persons exert power through projecting an appearance of superiority through the claim to complete self-sufficiency. Such autonomy is what Sennett calls an authority without love.[8]

This analysis of the evolution of personal relationships of authority may help us understand more clearly how church congregations and their clergy preach a gospel of partnership and yet continue to function as households of domination and subordination. This may also help us to base the partnering relationships of good housekeeping on an authority of freedom that responds to people's need for solidarity and care by empowering them through a relationship of mutuality.

Authority in congregations.   It seems to me that paternalism is a predominant pattern of authority in congregations. Paternalism can be an authority of false love that uses people's need for strength and assurance to dominate them through a relationship of dependence. It allows the clergy and other church leaders to continue to use the vocabulary and images of the patriarchal traditions, even though much of that basis for authority has disappeared. Even when persons exercise power as domination over others, they are able to use the language of fatherly caring to evoke feelings and responses of dependence. Thus church leaders can exercise the caring, nurturing, serving tasks of ministry without any threat to their leadership positions. They often are firmly in control of which groups meet and what curriculum they will use, even when there is no need for such care.

Persons need the kind of support that seeks to eliminate dependence, so that persons can care for themselves and others. They do not need care that continues to make them dependent, uncertain, and needy. For instance, it would be paternalistic to use the authority of one's knowledge and expertise to keep people dependent by refusing to preach or teach in such a way that a congregation has the opportunity of understanding and acting out the biblical story. When they are only handed a message rather than encouraged to seek it out themselves through group story and action, they remain dependent on the messenger and do not learn to carry out the ministry of the Word together with others. An extreme form of paternalistic authority would be offering to care for people as a father while carrying out many actions and policies that hurt them and keep them dependent.

The opposite extreme is autonomous authority, which projects an image of strength by appearing to be totally self-sufficient and invulnerable: needed by others but never needing others. This form of individualism is actually a valued and envied trait in white Western society. It is small wonder, therefore, that we seem to forget that all persons are interdependent. Growth in self-dependence is part of a maturing process that leads to full interdependence. Self-dependence is not an end in itself, either for those in ministry or for any other group of persons.[9]

In preaching or teaching, an autonomous relationship of authority with the listeners would most likely involve a display of the speaker's skills and knowledge in such a way that the person appears self-possessed and all-knowing. The bond of authority is formed through this image of superiority, in which everyone assumes the speaker is so powerful and full of wisdom that he or she cannot be challenged openly. This may reinforce a sense of inferiority and dependency among many of the listeners. They, in turn, withdraw from any attempt to develop a healthy independence of thought and action in the life of the community.

Although all persons need to develop self-dependence in their lives, subjection to autonomous behavior by pastors, employers, or government officials is more likely to reinforce feelings of inferiority and dependence. Therefore, the exercise of autonomous authority is not a creative alternative for ministry because it leads persons to deny their co-responsibility with God for their neighbor and for the world. Nor is paternalism helpful to the life and growth of the Christian community. Paternalistic authority continues the use of patriarchal imagery to justify the need for laypersons, and especially women, to remain dependent. In my view an alternative paradigm of authority that would foster interdependence in a household of freedom is partnership.

Building Up the Household

Partnership is an authority of freedom that uses people's need for solidarity and care to empower them through a relationship of mutuality. This would not be the only alternative to forms of paternalistic and autonomous authority. Yet it seems to me that bonds of assent based on partnership would be more responsive to God's actions in freely becoming partner with humanity, as well as the actions of Jesus in reaching out to restore human wholeness and community. In my books on partnership I describe it as a new focus of relationship in Jesus Christ that sets us free for others.[10] Like faith, partnership—*koinōnia*—is a relationship of trust with God and others that comes to us as a gift of Christ's love. Like faith it is "caught, not taught." *Koinōnia* is a word used frequently in the New Testament for sharing with someone in something, and it usually stresses a common bond in Jesus Christ that establishes mutual community. The emphasis is on a two-sided relationship of giving or receiving, participation or community (1 Cor. 10:16–17).

Strengthening partnership. In this new focus of relationship there is continuing commitment and common struggle in interaction with a wider community context. Such relationships happen as a gift; nevertheless, we know that commitment is more likely to grow where there is responsibility, vulnerability, equality, and trust among those who share diversity of gifts and resources. Because partnerships are living relationships that share the "already/not yet" character of God's new household, they are always in process and never finished as they draw us together in common struggle and work, involving risk, continuing growth, and hopefulness in moving toward a goal or purpose transcending the group. By definition, partnership involves growing interdependence in relation to God, persons, and creation. Interaction with a wider community of persons, social structures, values, and beliefs helps to provide support, correctives, and negative feedback. There is never complete equality in such a dynamic relationship, but a pattern of equal regard and mutual acceptance of different gifts among partners is essential.

Authority in partnership grows in a community when people take time to be partners with one another. In preaching, this might mean that mutuality would be developed by group Bible study in preparation for the sermon. The sermon in turn would be a sharing of community action, insight, and questioning. Rather than providing answers to what the congregation should believe and do, it would make use of the preacher's theological training and gifts to lift up the ongoing life of that congregation as part of God's continuing action. The stories of the participants could become the vehicles of biblical interpretation as the community discovers its mutual ministry of preaching.

Looking at these various alternative relational bonds of authority, we can see that paternalism is a pale imitation of the old patriarchal paradigm of authority *over* community. Yet in our society it has become a means of covering up alienation and loss of meaning with empty rhetoric and family clichés.[11] In the church it is an invitation to the sin of dependence and immaturity in faith and action. Autonomy is also not helpful in building up households of freedom. As a rebellion against dependence by claiming egoistic authority *outside of* community, it has led to equally disastrous results for the health of technological society. In the church it is also an invitation to the sin of pride and selfishness masked in the rhetoric of objectivity and excellence. Even though the glimpses of partnership as authority *in* community are few and far between, they are a genuine invitation to the freedom of Jesus Christ, whose love and acceptance sets us free to bear our own burdens and those of our neighbors in mutual housekeeping (Gal. 6:2).

Subverting structures. Many persons are concerned about how we can develop alternative structures of authority that move beyond those imaged in patriarchal forms of domination. While still living in these forms of relationship, we can, nevertheless, make use of the insights of the social sciences to help subvert these forms and to open up the possibility for more persons to find space in new households of freedom. To live in the present setting but to be constantly living out of an alternative future reality is to be *bi-cultural.*[12] This is a survival skill for anyone who wishes to participate in God's housekeeping chores. By knowing the social structures and psychological dynamics of the old house of bondage, we can work to subvert those structures and to limit their power in our lives and institutions. Subversion is most certainly one way of standing against the powers in this time before the full realization of God's eschatological household.

In the second part of his book, Richard Sennett is helpful in providing some psychosocial clues to the dynamics of authority For instance, it is possible to increase democracy and participa tion in an organization even when the structures are paternalistic and hierarchical by *disrupting the links* in the top-down chain of command.[13] This type of action may appear to cause trouble or "disorder," but it results in challenging and opening up organizational structures and attitudes so that people are better able to see the way things function and to understand what is going on. Authority as domination works through a chain of command from top to bottom. It works most effectively when the right to exercise power is unquestioned and the structures of the organization are assumed but not understood. If we are to avoid either anarchy or co-option into the system of domination, we need to develop strategies of disruption that reflect our bi-cultural vision.

Sennett suggests a few strategies that we might want to try.[14] In discussions with persons in authority it is important to require the "active voice." An order that is couched in terms of "It has been decided," needs to be explained in terms of who and why, so the decision may be questioned. A second suggestion is that the "assumed categories" or roles in which persons are placed need to be discussed. Perhaps there are other persons who need to be involved in a particular decision; perhaps there are other ways of carrying out decisions. In congregations there is certainly the possibility of doing this, rather than assuming that decency and order require unquestioned interpretation of the church order and traditions. Just because the church council has the authority to decide if the congregation will minister to women and children in crisis does not mean that they should make that decision without consulting those with experience of victimization or of intervention and counseling.

Two other important ways of disrupting the accustomed chain of command are that of "role exchange" and of "challenging paternalism." Role exchange disrupts the order of things because those in charge take on "subordinate tasks" through rotation and temporary inequality. I used to do this as a pastor in the East Harlem Protestant Parish. I would share in tasks of cleaning and typing so that the janitor and secretary could share in teaching, worship, and calling. I learned more about what it really takes to keep a church running, and my partners learned more about their own gifts for ministry.

Challenging paternalism happens as persons question the assumption that a particular action is really helpful and nourishing. In the church there are many promises of nurture and care that need to be challenged if they leave persons more dependent. For instance, the practice of giving out food and money without acting to change the situation that is causing the person's need for free food may need to be challenged. People prefer service or ministry that is empowering, that helps them gain the ability to care for themselves. Although direct aid is needed in emergency, it sometimes becomes a way of increasing dependence and subordination of the poor and of increasing false feelings of superiority among the rich. Reflecting critically on our own actions as well as those of others may help challenge many of our paternalistic assumptions about service and doing good.[15]

None of these are very dramatic ways of subverting the church into being the church, but they represent a beginning step in creating space for new household relationships to spring up. A household of freedom has no one structure or shape; it simply represents the two or three—or two or three thousand—gathered in Christ's name and seeking to participate in Christ's continuing housekeeping ministry for the world. Often these households are found within established congregations in the form of sanctuary churches, basic Christian communities, or shalom communities working for justice and peace. The ministry of such congregations is crucial in a society where religion is often a tool of "political messianism."[16]

But just as often, households of freedom can be glimpsed among those who form the *paroikia:* those outside the house of the church who come together around the needs of the oppressed and God's good housekeeping agenda. Such groups do not consider themselves separate churches, so they are not what would be called "sects" in classical sociology. Nevertheless they have the qualities of other such *paroikia* groups.[17] They have a distinct identity whose source is solidarity with the poor, the marginal, the dominated of society. Their internal coherence stems not from hierarchical structuring but from commitment to the task of struggle for change against the web of oppressions in which our world is engulfed. They make sense of the present situations of suffering and victimization by an appeal to a vision of a new household in which all persons will be treated as full human beings.

An example of this is the development of "women-church" groups. These groups understand the early egalitarian Christian community as a prototype for their life together, but they take on as many shapes and varieties as there are men and women who take part in the gatherings. Elisabeth Fiorenza describes women-church as "a feminist movement of self-identified women and women-identified men [which] transcends all traditional man-made denominational lines" and is committed to solidarity with the most despised women.[18]

These groups are particularly popular among Roman Catholic women because of their exclusion from ordination and decision making in that church.[19] But they provide a supportive community for women of all confessions who find that they are constantly ignored, put down, and excluded by the language and actions of their own congregations. Some have developed *Womanguides* for more inclusive readings, as well as a book of liturgy for *Women-Church*, both edited by Rosemary Ruether.[20] These groups are attempting to build up the household of freedom by focusing on those who constituted the bottom of the old house of bondage.

Authority from the Bottom

This is the major clue to finding our way into a new metaphor for relationships of authority in community. The clue is not some form of strict mathematical equality, for relationships of authority and power are constantly changing as they are lived out in human interactions. Rather, it is the foundation of authority that is built up from the bottom rather than established from the top down. In a speech delivered to a Hispanic audience in 1984, Jesse Jackson expressed it this way:

> When the black and Hispanic foundation comes together, everyone above has to adjust. We are not the bottom of this society where things end up. We are the foundation—where everything begins.[21]

God's option for the poor and marginal people, the homeless nobodies, sends us to look among those people to find how God's power is at work in the world. We discover that the bottom line for a new household of freedom is those who are not free. Welcoming them into the household causes a major shift in the way that we see reality. It causes a paradigm shift toward an inclusive authority of partnership or *koinōnia*. In solidarity with those at the bottom we join in expectant action, knowing that the first signs of God's household are already among us as we welcome one another.

Coming home again. The black women's ensemble Sweet Honey in the Rock sings a song that begins, "We all, every one of us, have to come home again."[22] Of course it attracted my attention because I have been thinking a lot about household metaphors. This one seemed to contradict the metaphor of Nelle Morton's book *The Journey Is Home*, not even to mention the familiar words from Thomas Wolfe that you can't go home again.[23] It most certainly is true that we can't go home again as long as the home we left is still part of the old relationships of patriarchy. I thought perhaps that going home in the song might refer to God's home in a manner similar to the spiritual "Oh, Freedom!" which ends with the words: "And before I'd be a slave, I'll be buried in my grave, and go home to my Lord and be free."

As I continued to listen to the women of Sweet Honey in the Rock, I heard another theme, however. They were singing of those who "were born on the bottom . . . lived on the bottom . . . grew up from the bottom" and declared that they'd never return to the bottom. And it seemed to me that they were singing about the foundation of the household of freedom. Only by coming home again to the bottom and building up the household in solidarity with all the wretched of the earth can we create all manner of different styles, types, and sizes of houses in which God's people will be free.

Clues to good housekeeping. Beginning from the bottom may provide us with some clues for the work of good housekeeping as we reinterpret the various ways described in chapter 1 that authority operates in our lives. We have already seen that it is not the feminist theologians who changed the paradigm. The paradigm was changed long ago through God's liberating activity in the exodus and resurrection. But the new reality of following a servant/ Lord and a God who suffers in solidarity with the people has always been transformed back into a pyramid with God stuck up on the top, no longer allowed to share with Christ in the story of the suffering people of God's world house.

The authority that comes to those who have the knowledge of the tradition was also locked up in the old house of domination. If the paradigm shifts, then that *authority through knowledge* can again be accessible to all those who want to participate in naming and changing their world. By using the "tools of the master" in the service of the oppressed, academic research and social analysis will become involved with reconstructing their "invisible past" as well as in analyzing ways to both fit and not fit into the dominant structure. The authority of knowledge will have a new source as well as a new task. As the words of the Sophia/Christ are heard with new ears, we turn to learn about the household of freedom from those who have discovered God in their midst in all ages.

From the perspective of the bottom, those whose cultural wisdom has been denied, ignored, or stolen from them find that they can still live out of the vision of God's new household. The memory of that future comes to them from such sources as Mary's

Magnificat in Luke 1:46–55, which declares that human life was not created for domination. It also comes to them out of their own stories, told and retold, about a past of holding on against tyranny and of a Housekeeper who intends the world to be otherwise. Those who believe this memory and this future will be maladjusted with the present as they join Mary's song about God's messianic politics. The *authority of wisdom* in this perspective becomes an authority that is born out of the experience of struggle, a wisdom at the disposal of the people as they cope with the present out of their living memories and hopes.

Those at the bottom must still cope with established forms of *structural authority* that justify their position at the bottom of the social, economic, and political structures of the world. Yet the basis of the new household of freedom is the refusal to worship these powers of domination and to worship God alone. Thus Jesus refused the temptation to jump from the pinnacle of the temple as a display of power and chose the way of obedient solidarity with the outcasts (Luke 4:9–13). In the same way, those who follow him find that they must reject the temptation of the "pinnacle complex" and work not to reverse the pyramid, so that they are on top, but rather to transform the pyramid so more persons gain access to the structures of decision making.

When many persons have access to participation in the structures of decision making, there is often an explosion of energy that makes it possible to build new households. This is what happened among the followers of Jesus. As poor and unorganized as they were, they discovered that it was possible to share together in feeding one another and in discovering new gifts for ministry. The charismatic authority of Jesus that enabled him to preach, heal, and work among the people was not something he kept to himself. Thus, for instance, in the story of the five thousand we hear that he involved the disciples and the people in the feeding (Mark 6:30–44). In a household of freedom the charisma of God's Spirit is recognized among the people, but those who lead find that their job description is one of *diakonos*, servant, and the job description is to work themselves out of a job. Charisma becomes a gift of empowerment for others rather than one for dominating and manipulating others.

On Maundy Thursday we do not have much trouble remembering what it means for at least one charismatic leader to work himself out of a job. Yet even here our congregations often avoid much of the meaning of that sacrifice by omitting John's powerful story of Mary anointing Jesus for his role as servant/housekeeper, and of Jesus acting out the meaning of that service in the washing of feet (John 12–13). In East Harlem we used to try to keep the liturgy as close to home as possible, so we celebrated the supper as a potluck with wine, fish, and bread and invited all the neighborhood. (Some of our street friends were regular attenders because of the abundant wine!) During the liturgy the pastors acted out the foot washing by becoming "shoeshine boys and girls," carefully polishing each person's shoes with a shoe-rag stole.

Recently some of us at Yale Divinity School who had read Elisabeth Fiorenza's powerful account of the anointing story as an act of "solidarity from below" wanted to celebrate "in memory of her" as part of the story of Maundy Thursday (Mark 14:9).[24] In the service we used dishcloths for the foot washing and put perfume on the cloths as a symbol of the anointing. Thus we celebrated the Last Supper as a domestic scene in which women and men gathered together and enacted the meaning of discipleship: "In memory of Jesus who washed the disciples' feet, and of Mary who anointed him as Messiah." The One who is the God's anointed continues to be with us among the poor, and the invitation to remember him, to remember her, to remember them is real.

In a discussion with Nicaraguan peasants about John 12:8, Ernesto Cardenal says in *The Gospel in Solentiname:*

> I think [Jesus] is saying that he's going away but that in place of him the poor are left. What that woman was doing with him, they'd have to do later with the poor, because he wasn't going to be there any longer, or rather, we are going to have his presence in the poor.[25]

That presence is a dangerous memory of the future. But it is offered to all who want to share in the good housekeeping chores of God's household.

Notes

Publication facts not supplied here appear in the Bibliography.

Preface and Acknowledgments

1. W. Eugene March, "Biblical Theology: Authority and the Presbyterians," *Journal of Presbyterian History* 59(2):114 (Summer 1981).
2. Margaret R. Miles, *Image as Insight*, p. 113. For Calvin's attitude toward women preachers, see Jane Dempsey Douglas, *Women, Freedom, and Calvin* (Westminster Press, 1985), pp. 93–94.
3. Joe Holland and Peter Henriot, *Social Analysis: Linking Faith and Justice*, rev. and enl. ed. (Orbis Books, 1984).
4. Hannah Arendt, *Between Past and Future*, pp. 91–93.
5. Gerhard Ebeling, *Word and Faith* (Fortress Press, 1963), pp. 363–364. Here and throughout, brackets indicate a word change in the quotation in order to make the language more inclusive.
6. Where possible, scriptural quotations follow the Revised Standard Version of the Bible as found in *An Inclusive-Language Lectionary*, Years A, B, C (John Knox Press, Pilgrim Press, Westminster Press, 1983, 1984, 1985). The use of inclusive language is consistent with a feminist perspective on authority. When the quotation is not found in the *Lectionary*, it will be quoted from the Revised Standard Version unchanged.

1. Authority of the Future

1. Peggy Ann Way, "An Authority of Possibility for Women in the Church," in *Women's Liberation and the Church*, ed. by Sarah Bentley Doely (Association Press, 1970), p. 91. Some of the material in this chapter was presented at the Trinity Institute Conference, "Love, the Foundation of Hope," New York, April 4, 1986, and will be published in English under

the title "Authority and Hope in Feminist Theology." It also is published in German in *Gottes Zukunft—Zukunft der Welt,* ed. by J. Deuser and others (Christian Kaiser Verlag, 1986), and is used here with permission.

2. Rosemary Radford Ruether, *Sexism and God-Talk: Toward a Feminist Theology,* pp. 12–13.

3. Gloria T. Hull, Patricia Bell Scott, and Barbara Smith, eds., *All the Women Are White, All the Blacks Are Men, but Some of Us Are Brave: Black Women's Studies* (Feminist Press, 1982), p. 49. Cf. Bell Hooks, *Feminist Theory: From Margin to Center* (South End Press, 1984), p. 8.

4. Beverly Wildung Harrison indicates that this phrase originates from the black oral/aural tradition. See La Frances Rodgers-Rose, ed., *The Black Woman* (Sage Publications, 1980), p. 10. Cited by Harrison in *Our Right to Choose,* p. 285.

5. Harrison, *Our Right to Choose,* p. 99.

6. Elisabeth Moltmann-Wendel and Jürgen Moltmann, *Humanity in God,* p. 11.

7. Elisabeth Schüssler Fiorenza, "Interpreting Patriarchal Traditions," in *The Liberating Word: A Guide to Nonsexist Interpretation of the Bible,* ed. by Letty M. Russell, pp. 49–51.

8. Phyllis Trible, unpublished lecture on "Patriarchy in Old Testament Theology" at Yale Divinity School, April 19, 1985.

9. Rosemary Ruether, "Feminist Theology in the Academy," *Christianity and Crisis* 45(3):61 (March 4, 1985).

10. Nicholas Lash, *A Matter of Hope: A Theologian's Reflection on the Thought of Karl Marx* (University of Notre Dame Press, 1981), p. 257.

11. Jürgen Moltmann, *Religion, Revolution, and the Future* (Charles Scribner's Sons, 1969), p. 77.

12. Beth E. Vanfossen, *The Structure of Social Inequality* (Little, Brown & Co., 1979), p. 141.

13. Ibid., p. 138. Vanfossen cites Max Weber's classic definition of power as "the chance of a [person] or a number of [persons] to realize their own will in communal action even against the resistance of others who are participating in the action." Cf. H. H. Gerth and C. Wright Mills, trans. and eds., *From Max Weber: Essays in Sociology* (Oxford University Press, 1946), p. 180.

14. Jo Ann Hackett, "In the Days of Jael: Reclaiming the History of Women in Ancient Israel," in *Immaculate and Powerful: The Female in Sacred Image and Social Reality,* ed. by Clarissa W. Atkinson, Constance H. Buchanan, and Margaret R. Miles (Beacon Press, 1985), p. 21.

15. Michelle Zimbalist Rosaldo, "Women, Culture, and Society: A Theoretical Overview," in *Woman, Culture, and Society,* ed. by M. Z. Rosaldo and Louise Lamphere (Stanford University Press, 1974), p. 21, n. 2.

16. Bengt Holmberg, *Paul and Power* (Fortress Press, 1978), pp. 130–135.

17. Richard Sennett, *Authority,* pp. 16–27.

18. Karl Barth, *Humanity of God* (John Knox Press, 1960), p. 51.

19. John E. Skinner, *The Meaning of Authority* (University Press of America, 1983), pp. 1–10, 68.

20. Moltmann-Wendel and Moltmann, *Humanity in God*, p. 112.

21. David H. Kelsey, *The Uses of Scripture in Recent Theology* (Fortress Press, 1975), p. 175.

22. Madeleine Boucher, "Authority-in-Community," *Mid-Stream* 21(3):415–416 (July 1982). Cf. Pheme Perkins, "Power in the New Testament," *Proceedings of the Thirty-second Annual Convention*, Catholic Theological Society of America, New York City, June 10–13, 1982; 37:83–89.

23. Arendt, "What Is Authority?", *Between Past and Future*, p. 122.

24. Ibid., pp. 104–120.

25. Fiorenza, *In Memory of Her*, p. 33.

26. Russell, *Growth in Partnership*, ch. 4, "Theology as Anticipation," pp. 87–109.

27. Margaret Walker, *Jubilee* (Houghton Mifflin Co., 1966).

28. Eleanor Traylor, "Music as Theme: The Blues Mode in the Works of Margaret Walker," in *Black Women Writers, 1950–1980*, p. 522.

29. Margaret Mitchell, *Gone with the Wind* (Macmillan Co., 1936). Cf. "Gone with the Wind Celebrates 50," by Richard Nalley, *United* 31(6):9 (June 1986).

30. Sharon H. Ringe, *Jesus, Liberation, and the Biblical Jubilee*, p. 56.

31. Ibid., pp. 16–17, 36.

32. Ibid., pp. 36, 50.

33. Ibid., p. 96.

34. Jürgen Moltmann, *God in Creation: A New Theology of Creation and the Spirit of God* (Harper & Row, 1985), p. 5.

35. Doreen Potter, "The Wall Is Down," 18 in *Break Not the Circle: Twenty New Hymns*, by Fred Kaan and Doreen Potter (Agape, 1975). I first noticed these words on the logo of the Stony Point Conference Center in Stony Point, N.Y.

2. Paradigms of Authority

1. The term "standpoint dependent" was used in an unpublished speech by Elizabeth Dodson Gray, "Changing Images of God," at a conference of the Synod of the Northeast, Presbyterian Church (U.S.A.), Stony Point Conference Center, November 8, 1985. It was quoted from Ronald M. Green, *Religious Reason: The Rational and Moral Basis of Religious Belief* (Oxford University Press, 1978).

2. Peter L. Berger and Thomas Luckmann, *The Social Construction of Reality: A Treatise in the Sociology of Knowledge* (Doubleday & Co., 1966). See also Jerry H. Gill, *On Knowing God* (Westminster Press, 1981), pp. 77–88.

3. James H. Cone, *God of the Oppressed* (Seabury Press, 1975), p. 16.

4. Gustavo Gutiérrez, *The Power of the Poor in History*, p. 200.

5. Rosemary Radford Ruether, "Feminist Interpretation: A Method of Correlation," in *Feminist Interpretation of the Bible*, ed. by Letty M. Russell, pp. 112–116.

6. Robert McAfee Brown, "What Is Contextual Theology?" in *Changing Contexts of Our Faith*, ed. by Letty M. Russell (Fortress Press, 1985), p. 81.

7. Gutiérrez, *Power of the Poor*, pp. 212–214.

8. Eugenia Collier, "Fields Watered with Blood: Myth and Ritual in the Poetry of Margaret Walker," in *Black Women Writers, 1950–1980*, ed. by Mari Evans, pp. 499–500; Ada Maria Isasi-Diaz, "Toward an Understanding of *Feminismo Hispano* in the U.S.A.," in *Women's Consciousness, Women's Conscience: A Reader in Feminist Ethics*, ed. by Barbara H. Andolsen and others (Winston Press, 1985), pp. 51–62.

9. McFague, *Metaphorical Theology*, pp. 79–83.

10. Letty M. Russell, "Authority and the Challenge of Feminist Interpretation," *Feminist Interpretation of the Bible*, pp. 137–146.

11. See Letty M. Russell, "Women and Ministry: Problem or Possibility?" in *Christian Feminism*, ed. by Judith L. Weidman, pp. 75–92.

12. Fiorenza, *Bread Not Stone*, p. xiv.

13. Elisabeth Moltmann-Wendel and Jürgen Moltmann, *Humanity in God*, p. 36.

14. Katharine Doob Sakenfeld, *Faithfulness in Action: Loyalty in Biblical Perspective* (Fortress Press, 1985), pp. 132–151. For a more extensive treatment of the rainbow image, see Judith L. Weidman, ed., *Christian Feminism*, pp. 80–92.

15. Martin Luther King, Jr., *Where Do We Go from Here: Chaos or Community?* (Beacon Press, 1967), p. 167.

16. Gordon D. Kaufman, *The Theological Imagination: Constructing the Concept of God* (Westminster Press, 1981), p. 11.

17. McFague, *Metaphorical Theology*, p. 83.

18. Bonnie Pedrotti Kittel, *Biblical Hebrew* (no publisher, 1978), p. 101; O. R. Sellers, "House," *The Interpreter's Dictionary of the Bible*, vol. 2, ed. by George A. Buttrick and others (Abingdon Press, 1962), p. 657.

19. John Koenig, *New Testament Hospitality: Partnership with Strangers as Promise and Mission* (Fortress Press, 1985).

20. Fiorenza, *In Memory of Her*, Parts 2 and 3, pp. 97–342. See also John H. Elliott, *A Home for the Homeless*; John G. Gager, *Kingdom and Community: The Social World of Early Christianity* (Prentice-Hall, 1975); Abraham J. Malherbe, *Social Aspects of Early Christianity* (Fortress Press, 2nd ed., 1983); Wayne A. Meeks, *The First Urban Christians: The Social World of the Apostle Paul* (Yale University Press, 1983); Gerhard Theissen, *Sociology of Early Palestinian Christianity* (Fortress Press, 1977).

21. Walter Brueggemann, *The Land: Place as Gift, Promise, and Challenge in Biblical Faith* (Fortress Press, 1977), pp. 3–6, 189.

22. Sharon H. Ringe, *Jesus, Liberation, and the Biblical Jubilee*, pp. 33–49. Cf. Letty M. Russell, "Partnership in New Creation," *Growth in Partnership*, pp. 15–38.

23. Jürgen Moltmann with M. Douglas Meeks, "The Liberation of Oppressors," in *Christianity and Crisis* 38(20):315–316 (Dec. 25, 1978).

24. Luise Schottroff, "Women as Followers of Jesus," in *The Bible and Liberation: Political and Social Hermeneutics*, ed. by Norman K. Gottwald (Orbis Books, 1983), pp. 418–427.

25. Schottroff, pp. 422–423.

26. Malherbe, *Social Aspects*, pp. 69–72; Fiorenza, *In Memory of Her*, p. 287; John G. Gager, "Social Description and Sociological Explanation in the Study of Early Christianity: A Review Article," in *The Bible and Liberation*, ed. by Norman K. Gottwald, pp. 431–440.

27. Fiorenza, *In Memory of Her*, pp. 289–294; Elliott, *A Home for the Homeless*, pp. 220–233.

28. Rudolf Bultmann, *Theology of the New Testament* (Charles Scribner's Sons, 1951), vol. 1, p. 353; L. Russell, *The Future of Partnership*, pp. 167–176.

29. Delores S. Williams, "Black Women's Literature and the Task of Feminist Theology," in *Immaculate and Powerful: The Female in Sacred Image and Social Reality*, ed. by Clarissa W. Atkinson, Constance H. Buchanan, and Margaret R. Miles (Beacon Press, 1985), pp. 101–102.

30. Nelle Morton, *The Journey Is Home*, pp. 152–155.

31. Hannah Arendt, *On Revolution* (Viking Press, 1965), p. 28.

3. Power of Naming

1. Clifford Geertz, "Religion as a Cultural System," in *Reader in Comparative Religion*, 2nd (rev.) ed., ed. by William Lessa and Evon Vogt (Harper & Row, 1972), pp. 204–216. Quoted by Carol P. Christ and Judith Plaskow, eds., *Womanspirit Rising: A Feminist Reader in Religion*, p. 2; see also p. 7.

2. See Letty M. Russell, "Inclusive Language and Power," *Religious Education* 80(4):582–602 (Fall 1985). Material from this article is used in chapter 3 with permission. For a more positive view of Psalm 8 see Letty M. Russell, *Becoming Human* (Westminster Press, 1982), pp. 35–47.

3. Joshua A. Fishman, "Whorfianism of the Third Kind: Ethnolinguistic Diversity as a Worldwide Societal Asset (The Whorfian Hypothesis: Varieties of Validation, Confirmation, and Disconfirmation II)," *Language in Society*, vol. 2 (1982), pp. 1–14. Cf. *Selected Writings of Edward Sapir in Language, Culture, and Personality*, ed. by David G. Mandelbaum (University of California Press, 1949); *Language, Thought, and Reality: Selected Writings of Benjamin Lee Whorf*, ed. by John B. Carroll (Technology Press, 1956).

4. Adrienne Rich, "Power and Danger: Works of a Common Woman (1977)," *On Lies, Secrets, and Silence: Selected Prose 1966–1978* (W. W. Norton & Co., 1979), p. 246.

5. Ibid., p. 256. Cf. also Audrey Lorde, "The Transformation of Silence Into Language and Action," *Sister Outsider: Speeches and Essays* (Crossing Press, 1984), pp. 40–44.

6. *Harvard Crimson*, Cambridge, Mass., 1971.

7. Ann Bodine, "Androcentrism in Prescriptive Grammar: Singular 'Theory', Sex-indefinite 'He,' and 'He or She,' " *Language and Society*, 4:129–146 (1975).

8. "Sex Differences in Language, Speech, and Nonverbal Communication: An Annotated Bibliography," in *Language and Sex: Difference and*

Dominance, ed. by Barrie Thorne and Nancy Henley (Newbury House Publishers, 1975), pp. 205–309; "Sex Similarities and Differences in Language, Speech, and Nonverbal Communication: An Annotated Bibliography," in *Language, Gender, and Society,* ed. by Cheris Kramarae, Barrie Thorne, and Nancy Henley (Newbury House Publishers, 1983), pp. 153–332.

9. Thorne and Henley, *Language and Sex,* p. ix. I am indebted to J. Shannon Clarkson, Ph.D. student in religious education and linguistics at Columbia Teachers College, for the resources in linguistic history and theory. Cf. "Language, Thought, and Social Justice," ed. by Shannon Clarkson, Task Force on Education Strategies for an Inclusive Church, Division of Education and Ministry, NCCC, N.Y., 1986.

10. Jean Baker Miller, *Toward a New Psychology of Women* (Beacon Press, 1976), p. 116; Elizabeth Janeway, *Powers of the Weak,* p. 109.

11. Anne Wilson Schaef, *Women's Reality: An Emerging Female System in the White Male Society* (Winston Press, 1981). Cf. *Language and Power,* ed. by Cheris Kramarae, Muriel Schulz, and William M. O'Barr (Sage Publications, 1984).

12. "Naming, Claiming, Changing: Sojourneys with Black Women," a lecture and workshop series of the Women's Theological Center, Boston, Mass., 1984–85.

13. Miles, *Image as Insight,* p. 20.

14. Trible, *God and the Rhetoric of Sexuality,* pp. 88–105.

15. Janeway, *Powers of the Weak,* p. 28.

16. Emily V. Gibbes and Valerie Russell, "Foreword," *The Liberating Word,* ed. by Letty M. Russell, p. 9. See *An Inclusive-Language Lectionary,* Years A, B, C (John Knox Press, Pilgrim Press, Westminster Press, 1983, 1984, 1985).

17. David H. Kelsey, *The Uses of Scripture in Recent Theology* (Fortress Press, 1975), pp. 167–175, 194.

18. Thomas S. Kuhn, *The Structure of Scientific Revolutions,* 2nd ed., enl. (University of Chicago Press, 1970), p. 175.

19. Kelsey, *Uses of Scripture,* pp. 170–175.

20. Letty M. Russell, "Authority and the Challenge of Feminist Interpretation," *Feminist Interpretation of the Bible,* pp. 137–146.

21. Margaret A. Farley, "Feminist Consciousness and the Interpretation of Scripture," in Russell, ed., *Feminist Interpretation of the Bible,* pp. 41–51.

22. Phyllis A. Bird, *The Bible as the Church's Book* (Westminster Press, 1982), pp. 107–108.

23. Ibid., pp. 33–37.

24. Virginia Ramey Mollenkott, *The Divine Feminine: The Biblical Imagery of God as Female* (Crossroad Publishing Co., 1983).

25 *Daughters of Sarah* 11(2) (March/April 1985), entire issue on the theme of "Inclusive Language: Imagery for God." Cf. *Union Seminary Quarterly Review,* 40(3)(1985), entire issue on the theme of "Religious Language."

26. Christ and Plaskow, eds., *Womanspirit Rising*, p. 3.

27. Walker, *The Color Purple*, pp. 165–168.

28. McFague, *Metaphorical Theology*, pp. 9, 145–152.

29. Robert Hamerton-Kelly, *God the Father: Theology and Patriarchy in the Teaching of Jesus* (Fortress Press, 1979), pp. 100–104.

30. Gordon D. Kaufman, *The Theological Imagination: Constructing the Concept of God* (Westminster Press, 1981), p. 14.

31. Mary Daly, *Gyn/Ecology: The Metaethics of Radical Feminism* (Beacon Press, 1978).

32. Mary Daly, *Beyond God the Father: Toward a Philosophy of Women's Liberation* (Beacon Press, 1973), p. 19. Cf. Carol P. Christ, "Why Women Need the Goddess: Phenomenological, Psychological, and Political Reflections," *Womanspirit Rising*, pp. 273–287.

33. Rosemary Ruether, "Feminist Theology in the Academy," *Christianity and Crisis* 45(3):57–62 (September 1985).

34. Morton, *The Journey Is Home*, pp. 147–175.

35. Daniel L. Migliore, *The Power of God* (Westminster Press, 1983), p. 34.

36. Ruether, *Sexism and God-Talk*, pp. 1–11.

37. Isabel Carter Heyward, *The Redemption of God: A Theology of Mutual Relation* (University Press of America, 1982), pp. 1–2; McFague, *Metaphorical Theology*, pp. 188–192.

38. Kristen E. Kvam, "Sophia, Christology, and Inclusive Language," unpublished STM thesis, Yale Divinity School, September 1, 1985. Cf. James D. G. Dunn, *Christology in the Making: A New Testament Inquiry Into the Origins of the Doctrine of the Incarnation* (Westminster Press, 1980), p. 176.

39. Joan Chamberlain Engelsman, *The Feminine Dimension of the Divine* (Westminster Press, 1979), pp. 74–75. Cf. also Robert L. Wilken, ed., *Aspects of Wisdom in Judaism and Early Christianity* (University of Notre Dame Press, 1975).

40. Raymond E. Brown, *The Gospel According to John I–XII* (Doubleday & Co., 1966), pp. cxxii–cxxv.

41. Fiorenza, *In Memory of Her*, p. 133.

42. Ibid., pp. 189–190. Fiorenza also cites John 1:1–14; Ephesians 2:14–16; Colossians 1:15–20; 1 Timothy 3:16; Hebrews 1:3; and 1 Peter 3:18, 22.

43. Dunn, *Christology in the Making*, pp. 197, 202–204. Quoted by Kvam, "Sophia," pp. 13–20.

44. Brown, *The Gospel According to John*, p. 520.

45. Ringe, *Jesus, Liberation, and the Biblical Jubilee*, p. 36.

46. Mollenkott, *The Divine Feminine*, pp. 60–68. See also Katharine Sakenfeld, "Feminine and Masculine Images of God in Scripture and Translation," in *The Word and Words: Beyond Gender in Theological and Liturgical Language*, ed. by William D. Watley (Princeton: Consultation on Church Union, 1983).

4. New House of Authority

1. Marie Augusta Neal, "Sociology and Sexuality: A Feminist Perspective," *Christianity and Crisis* 39(8):118–122 (May 14, 1979).

2. Bill J. Leonard, "Forgiving Eve," *Christian Century*, Nov. 7, 1984, pp. 1038–1040.

3. Judith L. Weidman, "Introduction," *Christian Feminism*, ed. by Judith Weidman, p. 3.

4. Mary Ann Tolbert, "Defining the Problem," in *The Bible and Feminist Hermeneutics* (Semeia 28), ed. by Mary Ann Tolbert (Scholars Press, 1983), p. 120.

5. Audrey Lorde, *Sister Outsider: Speeches and Essays* (Crossing Press, 1984), pp. 110–113.

6. Katie Cannon, panelist on "Creating New Reality," Asian Women Theologians Conference, Stony Point, N.Y., June 1, 1986, unpublished.

7. Lillian Smith, *Killers of the Dream* (W. W. Norton & Co., 1949), pp. 27, 29.

8. Katie Cannon, in *God's Fierce Whimsy*, by The Mud Flower Collective, p. 57.

9. Eleanor Traylor, "Music as Theme: The Blues Mode in the Works of Margaret Walker," in *Black Women Writers, 1950–1980*, ed. by Mari Evans, p. 522.

10. Georges Casalis, *Correct Ideas Don't Fall from the Skies: Elements for an Inductive Theology* (Orbis Books, 1984, 1977), p. 6.

11. Raymond E. Brown, *The Gospel According to John I–XII* (Doubleday & Co., 1966), pp. 114–125; I. Howard Marshall, *The Gospel of Luke* (Wm. B. Eerdmans Publishing Co., 1978), pp. 719–726.

12. George V. Pixley, *God's Kingdom: A Guide for Bible Study* (Orbis Books, 1981), p. 75.

13. Edward Farley, *Ecclesial Reflection: An Anatomy of Theological Methods* (Fortress Press, 1982), p. 5.

14. Ibid., p. 117.

15. Ibid., p. 165.

16. Cf. Harvey Cox, *Religion in the Secular City: Toward a Post-Modern Theology* (Simon & Schuster, 1984), Part I: "Praying for the Children at the Gate: The Conservative Critique of Modern Theology," pp. 29–84.

17. Beverly Wildung Harrison, *Making the Connections*, ed. by Carol S. Robb (Beacon Press, 1985); Margaret R. Miles, *Image as Insight;* Rosemary Radford Ruether, *Sexism and God-Talk;* Juan Luis Segundo, *Liberation of Theology* (Orbis Books, 1976); Cornel West, *Prophesy Deliverance! An Afro-American Revolutionary Christianity* (Westminster Press, 1982).

18. Lorde, *Sister Outsider*, p. 112.

19. Delores Williams, "Women's Oppression and Lifeline Politics in Black Women's Religious Narratives," *Journal of Feminist Studies in Religion* 1(2):58–71 (Fall 1985).

20. Phyllis Trible, "Depatriarchalizing in Biblical Interpretation," *Journal of the American Academy of Religion* 41:30–48 (1973).

21. Katharine Doob Sakenfeld, "Feminist Uses of Biblical Materials," in *Feminist Interpretation of the Bible*, ed. by L. Russell, p. 55.

22. Dietrich Bonhoeffer, *Letters and Papers from Prison*, enl. ed., ed. by Eberhard Bethge (Macmillan Publishing Co., 1972), p. 17.

23. Leonardo Boff, *Church: Charism and Power: Liberation Theology and the Institutional Church* (Crossroad Publishing Co., 1985), pp. 59, 125–130.

24. Sharon H. Ringe, "A Gentile Woman's Story"; J. Cheryl Exum, " 'Mother in Israel': A Familiar Story Reconsidered"; T. Drorah Setel, "Prophets and Pornography: Female Sexual Imagery in Hosea"; Susan Brooks Thistlethwaite, "Every Two Minutes: Battered Women and Feminist Interpretation," in *Feminist Interpretation of the Bible*, ed. by L. Russell, pp. 55–107.

25. Fiorenza, *Bread Not Stone*, p. 86.

26. Phyllis Trible, *Texts of Terror: Literary-Feminist Readings of Biblical Narratives* (Fortress Press, 1984).

27. Elsa Tamez, "Women and the Bible," *Lucha*, New York Circus 9(3):54–64 (June 1985).

28. Jean C. Lambert, "An 'F Factor'? The New Testament in Some White, Feminist, Christian Theological Construction," *Journal of Feminist Studies in Religion* 1(2):103 (Fall 1985).

29. Doris Ellzey Blasoff, "We Are Gathered," *Everflowing Streams: Songs for Worship*, ed. by Ruth Duck and Michael G. Bausch (1981), p. 2. Cf. Ruth Duck, "Lead On, O Cloud of Yahweh," p. 77.

30. Morton, *The Journey Is Home*, p. xix. Nelle Morton uses Ruth Duck's song as the theme of her collection of essays. See also the powerful rendition of this theme from a black woman's perspective in *Home Girls: A Black Feminist Anthology*, ed. by Barbara Smith (Kitchen Table: Women of Color Press, 1983). "*Home Girls* provides a means to know yourself and to be known, that between its pages you start to feel at home. Because in the end, there is nothing more important to us than home" (p. liv).

31. Some of the material in this section, delivered at Trinity Institute (1986) and published in *Gottes Zukunft—Zukunft der Welt*, 1986, is used here with permission (see chapter 1, note 1). See Jürgen Moltmann, *The Crucified God: The Cross of Christ as the Foundation and Criticism of Christian Theology* (Harper & Row, 1974), pp. 171–172.

32. Fiorenza, "The Will to Choose or to Reject: Continuing Our Critical Work," in *Feminist Interpretation of the Bible*, ed. by L. Russell, p. 128.

33. Ibid., p. 132.

34. Fiorenza, *Bread Not Stone*, pp. xiv–xvii. In a review of *In Memory of Her*, Mary Rose D'Angelo points out that Fiorenza has not abandoned the Bible but has appealed to the authority of the reconstructed movements of early Christian community rather than to the biblical texts themselves. See "A Feminist Reading of Scripture," *The Ecumenist* 23:86–89 (Sept.–Oct. 1985).

35. *Bread Not Stone*, p. xiv.

36. Ruether, "Feminist Interpretation: A Method of Correlation," in *Feminist Interpretation of the Bible*, ed. by L. Russell, p. 117; see also *Sexism and God-Talk*, pp. 22–27.

37. Ruether, *Sexism and God-Talk*, p. 254.

38. Ruether, *Womanguides*, p. xi.

39. Carter Heyward, "An Unfinished Symphony of Liberation: The Radicalization of Christian Feminism Among White U.S. Women," *Journal of Feminist Studies in Religion* 1(1):104 (Spring 1985).

40. Alice Walker, *The Color Purple*, pp. 166–168.

41. Alice Walker, "If God Ever Listened," *Horizons* #840307, National Public Radio, 1984.

42. Alice Walker, *In Search of Our Mothers' Gardens: Womanist Prose* (Harcourt Brace Jovanovich, 1983), p. 17.

43. Ibid., p. 252.

44. Jürgen Moltmann, *God in Creation* (Harper & Row, 1985), p. 5.

45. Krister Stendahl, "God Worries About Every Ounce of Creation," *Harvard Divinity Bulletin* 9(5):5 (June/July 1979).

46. Jürgen Moltmann and M. Douglas Meeks, "The Liberation of Oppressors," *Christianity and Crisis* 38(20):316 (Dec. 25, 1978).

47. Katie Geneva Cannon, "Rage and Redemption: Experiences of the Black Church," April 26, 1985, Women's Theological Center, Boston, Mass. See also Paula Giddings, *When and Where I Enter: The Impact of Black Women on Race and Sex in America* (William Morrow & Co., 1984), pp. 289–290.

48. Dorothee Soelle with Shirley A. Cloyes, *To Work and to Love: A Theology of Creation* (Fortress Press, 1984), p. 103.

5. Household, Power, and Glory

1. An earlier version of this chapter, entitled "People and the Powers," appears in the *Princeton Seminary Bulletin*, vol. 8, no. 1 (February 1987), and is used by permission.

2. Kim Yong-Bock, "Messiah and Minjung: Discerning Messianic Politics Over Against Political Messianism," *Minjung Theology: People as the Subjects of History*, ed. by the Commission on Theological Concerns of the Christian Conference of Asia, p. 186.

3. Ibid., pp. 183–193. See Rubem A. Alves, *A Theology of Human Hope* (Corpus Books, 1969); Allan Aubrey Boesak, *Farewell to Innocence: A Socio-Ethical Study on Black Theology and Power* (Orbis Books, 1977), "The Kairos Document," Sept. 13, 1985, published as *Challenge to the Church: A Theological Comment on the Political Crisis in South Africa*, by Theology in Global Context, Stony Point Center, Stony Point, N.Y.

4. Peggy Billings with Moon Tong Hwan, Han Wan Sang, Son Myong Gul, Pharis Harvey, *Fire Beneath the Frost* (Friendship Press, 1984), p. 9. See also *Minjung Theology*, pp. 35, 142–143, and Suh Kwang Sun David, "Theology of Story Telling: A Theology by Minjung," *Ministerial Formation*, Geneva: Programme on Theological Education, WCC, 31:10–22 (September 1985)

5. Alves, *Theology of Human Hope*, pp. 131–132.

6. Rosemary Ruether, "A Religion for Women: Sources and Strategies," *Christianity and Crisis* 39(19):309 (Dec. 10, 1979). Cf. L. Russell, "Minjung Theology in Women's Perspective," in forthcoming book of critical reflections on *Minjung Theology*, ed. by Jung Young Lee (Orbis Books, 1987).

7. Yong-Bock, "Messiah and Minjung," p. 191.

8. I am indebted in this interpretation to my husband, the late Johannes (Hans) Christiaan Hoekendijk. Some scholars doubt whether this parable was actually told by Jesus, yet the ideas are consistent with his continuing identification with God's hospitality for all outcasts and those at the bottom of the patriarchal pyramid (Mark 9:37, 41; 10:15). Cf. Joachim Jeremias, *The Parables of Jesus* (Charles Scribner's Sons, 1956), p. 144.

9. Krister Stendahl, " 'When you pray, pray in this manner. . .'—a Bible study," in *The Kingdom on Its Way: Meditations and Music for Mission*, RISK Book Series (Geneva: World Council of Churches, 1980), pp. 40–41.

10. Ahn Byung-Mu, "Jesus and the Minjung in the Gospel of Mark," *Minjung Theology*, pp. 138–152; Bell Hooks, *Feminist Theory: From Margin to Center* (South End Press, 1984), p. 161.

11. Gustavo Gutiérrez, *The Power of the Poor in History*, p. 200. The image of Zacchaeus is important for those who are prosperous and think there is nothing they can do to participate in the messianic story. Cf. Elizabeth Randall, "The Rich Young Ruler and Zacchaeus: Changing Paradigms," unpublished paper for Issues in Liberation Theology, Yale Divinity School, 1985.

12. Bernice Johnson Reagon, "Coalition Politics Turning the Century,' in *Home Girls: A Black Feminist Anthology*, ed. by Barbara Smith (Kitchen Table: Women of Color Press, 1983), pp. 356–357.

13. See L. Russell, "Reflections from a First World Perspective," in *Doing Theology in a Divided World*, ed. by Virginia Fabella and Sergio Torres (Orbis Books, 1985), pp. 206–211.

14. Marta Benavides, untitled speech at Yale Divinity School, October 5, 1985. According to E. Fiorenza (*In Memory of Her*, p. 135), this is one of the sayings from the Sophia tradition. There is violence against the envoys of Sophia, who proclaim her unlimited goodness and welcome all her children.

15. Walter Wink, *Naming the Powers: The Language of Power in the New Testament*, vol. 1, *The Powers* (Fortress Press, 1984), pp. 7–8. See also vol. 2, *Unmasking the Powers* (1986) and vol. 3, *Engaging the Powers* (publication date unknown), and the forthcoming book by J.P.M. Walsh, *The Mighty from Their Thrones: Power in the Biblical Tradition* (Fortress Press, 1987). Cf. Elisabeth Schüssler Fiorenza, *The Book of Revelation: Justice and Judgment* (Fortress Press, 1985), p. 4. "If, as Ernst Kasemann has pointed out, the central question of Jewish and Christian apocalyptic theology is the question of power, then Rev. is clearly an articulation of such a theology."

16. Wink, *Naming the Powers*, p. 10.

17. Ibid., pp. 5, 7–8.

18. Marcus Barth, *Ephesians: Introduction, Translation, and Commentary on Chapters 1-3* (Doubleday & Co., 1974), p. 174.

19. Letty M. Russell, *Imitators of God: A Study Book on Ephesians* (Women's Division, United Methodist Church, 1984), p. 120.

20. Paula Cooey, "The Power of Transformation and the Transformation of Power," *Journal of Feminist Studies in Religion*, 1(1):23-36 (Spring 1985).

21. Hannah Arendt, *The Human Condition* (University of Chicago Press, 1958), pp. 200-201.

22. Douglas P. Biklen, *Community Organizing: Theory and Practice* (Prentice-Hall, 1983), pp. 21-28.

23. Janeway, *Powers of the Weak*, pp. 157-185.

24. Janice G. Raymond, "Female Friendship and Feminist Ethics," in *Women's Consciousness, Women's Conscience*, ed. by B. Andolsen and others (Winston Press, 1985), pp. 164-167. Cf. Raymond's *A Passion for Friends: Toward a Philosophy of Female Affection* (Beacon Press, 1986).

25. Walter Wink, "Idol Time," *The Auburn News*, Auburn Theological Seminary, New York (Fall 1982), pp. 2, 5.

26. Dorothee Soelle, *Choosing Life* (Fortress Press, 1981), p. 7.

27. Graham Greene, *The Power and the Glory* (Viking Press, 1940).

28. Rosemary Radford Ruether, *To Change the World: Christology and Cultural Criticism* (Crossroad Publishing Co., 1981), pp. 55-56.

29. Sharon H. Ringe, *Jesus, Liberation, and the Biblical Jubilee*, p. 75.

30. Ibid., p. 4. Ringe notes two reversals in the parable: the domestic imagery for God, and the leaven as a positive symbol, rather than a substance banned from the household at Passover (Ex. 12:14-20).

31. John Koenig, *New Testament Hospitality* (Fortress Press, 1985). He quotes Sverre Aalen as saying that the kingdom is not so much reigning activity but "a community, a house, an area where goods of salvation are available and received," p. 42. See Aalen, " 'Reign' and 'House' in the Kingdom of God in the Gospels," *New Testament Studies* 8:223 (1962).

32. Fiorenza, *In Memory of Her*, pp. 118-120.

33. "Oikia/oikos. . . ," *Theological Dictionary of the New Testament*, vol. 5, ed. by Gerhard Friedrich (Wm. B. Eerdmans Publishing Co., 1967), pp. 131-138.

34. John H. Elliott, *A Home for the Homeless*, pp. 165-266.

35. See the forthcoming book by M. Douglas Meeks, *The Doctrine of God in Political Economy*. Meeks has written extensively about "God as economist," making use of the household metaphor in terms of the need for reimaging God's justice in economic and political structures.

36. Adrienne Rich, "Natural Resources," *The Dream of a Common Language: Poems 1974-1977* (W. W. Norton & Co., 1978), p. 67.

6. Good Housekeeping

1. Some of the material in this chapter was published as "Authority in Mutual Ministry," *Quarterly Review* 6(1):10-23 (Spring 1986), and is reprinted in modified form, with permission.

2. "Minutes of the Standing Commission on Faith and Order," World Council of Churches, Crete, 1984, Faith and Order, Paper #121, pp. 33–52.

3. Letty M. Russell, "Women and Unity: Problem or Possibility?" *Mid-Stream* 21(3):298–304 (July 1982).

4. See also L. Russell, *The Future of Partnership.*

5. Sennett, *Authority,* pp. 16–27.

6. Marie Marshall Fortune, *Sexual Violence: The Unmentionable Sin* (Pilgrim Press, 1983). Cf. R. Ruether, "Politics and the Family: Recapturing a Lost Issue," *Christianity and Crisis* 40(15):261–266 (Sept. 29, 1980).

7. Sennett, *Authority,* pp. 50–83.

8. Ibid., pp. 84–124.

9. Carol Gilligan, *In a Different Voice* (Harvard University Press, 1982), p. 74.

10. Russell, *Growth in Partnership,* pp. 22–29.

11. Rosemary Radford Ruether, "Family, in a Dim Light," *Christianity and Crisis* 43(11):263–266 (June 27, 1983).

12. See Gayraud S. Wilmore, "Religion and American Politics: Beyond the Veil," in *Churches in Struggle: Liberation Theologies and Social Change in North America,* ed. by William K. Tabb (Monthly Review Press, 1986), pp. 321–325.

13. Sennett, *Authority,* pp. 165–190.

14. Ibid., pp. 175–190. Cf. Letty M. Russell, "Women and Ministry: Problem or Possibility?" in *Christian Feminism,* ed. by Judith L. Weidman, pp. 75–94.

15. A helpful book for analyzing social issues is Joe Holland and Peter Henriot, *Social Analysis: Linking Faith and Justice,* rev. and enl. ed. (Orbis Books, 1984).

16. William K. Tabb, ed., *Churches in Struggle: Liberation Theologies and Social Change in North America,* pt. 5, "Political Action and the Mission of the Church," pp. 268–325.

17. John H. Elliott, *A Home for the Homeless,* pp. 102–106. Elliott is discussing "sect" characteristics in 1 Peter.

18. Elisabeth Schüssler Fiorenza, *Bread Not Stone,* pp. 7–8.

19. Marga Buhrig, "The Role of Women in the Ecumenical Dialogue," *Concilium* 182 (6/1985): Feminist Theology, p. 97. Buhrig says, "A growing number of women within and outside the churches are no longer content to accept office in an unchanged and patriarchally structured Church. They are looking for new models (e.g., the 'Church of Women') summed up in expressions such as 'participatory,' 'communicative,' 'partnership,' 'non-hierarchical,' and 'reciprocity of ministries.'" See also The Mud Flower Collective, *God's Fierce Whimsy.*

20. Rosemary Radford Ruether, *Womanguides: Readings Toward a Feminist Theology; Women-Church: Theology and Practice of Feminist Liturgical Communities* (Harper & Row, 1986).

21. Jesse Jackson, "Converging Interests and a New Direction," speech delivered on April 16, 1984, quoted in "Somewhere Over the Rainbow" by Sheila D. Collins, in *Churches in Struggle,* ed. by William K. Tabb, p. 315.

22. Bernice Johnson Reagon, Song Talk Publishing Co., *Sweet Honey in*

the Rock: "We All. . . Every One of Us" (Chicago: Flying Fish Records, 1983).

23. Morton, *The Journey Is Home*, pp. xviii–xix.

24. Fiorenza, *In Memory of Her*, pp. 153, xiii–xiv. Cf. Sharon H. Ringe, *Jesus, Liberation, and the Biblical Jubilee*, pp. 63–71.

25. *The Gospel in Art by the Peasants of Solentiname*, ed. by Philip and Sally Scharper (Orbis Books, 1984), p. 44.

Bibliography

Arendt, Hannah. *Between Past and Future*. New York: Viking Press, 1968.

Christ, Carol P., and Judith Plaskow, eds. *Womanspirit Rising: A Feminist Reader in Religion*. New York: Harper & Row, 1979.

Elliott, John H. *A Home for the Homeless*. Philadelphia: Fortress Press, 1981.

Evans, Mari, ed. *Black Women Writers, 1950–1980: A Critical Evaluation*. Garden City, N.Y.: Doubleday & Co., Anchor Books, 1984.

Fiorenza, Elisabeth Schüssler. *Bread Not Stone: The Challenge of Feminist Biblical Interpretation*. Boston: Beacon Press, 1984.

———. *In Memory of Her: A Feminist Theological Reconstruction of Christian Origins*. New York: Crossroad Publishing Co., 1983.

Gutiérrez, Gustavo. *The Power of the Poor in History*. Maryknoll, N.Y.: Orbis Books, 1983.

Harrison, Beverly Wildung. *Our Right to Choose: Toward a New Ethic of Abortion*. Boston: Beacon Press, 1983.

Janeway, Elizabeth. *Powers of the Weak*. New York: William Morrow & Co., Quill Paperbacks, 1981.

McFague, Sallie. *Metaphorical Theology*. Philadelphia: Fortress Press, 1982.

Miles, Margaret R. *Image as Insight: Visual Understanding in Western Christianity and Secular Culture*. Boston: Beacon Press, 1985.

Minjung Theology: People as the Subjects of History. Ed. by the Commission on Theological Concerns of the Christian Conference of Asia. Maryknoll, N.Y.: Orbis Books, 1983.

Moltmann-Wendel, Elisabeth, and Jürgen Moltmann. *Humanity in God*. New York: Pilgrim Press, 1983.

Morton, Nelle. *The Journey Is Home*. Boston: Beacon Press, 1985.

The Mud Flower Collective. *God's Fierce Whimsy: Christian Feminism and Theological Education*. New York: Pilgrim Press, 1985.

Ringe, Sharon H. *Jesus, Liberation, and the Biblical Jubilee: Image for Ethics and Christology*. Philadelphia: Fortress Press, 1985.

Ruether, Rosemary Radford. *Sexism and God-Talk: Toward a Feminist Theology*. Boston: Beacon Press, 1983.

———. *Womanguides: Readings Toward a Feminist Theology*. Boston: Beacon Press, 1985.

Russell, Letty M. *The Future of Partnership*. Philadelphia: Westminster Press, 1979.

———. *Growth in Partnership*. Philadelphia: Westminster Press, 1981.

———, ed. *Feminist Interpretation of the Bible*. Philadelphia: Westminster Press, 1985.

———. *The Liberating Word: A Guide to Nonsexist Interpretation of the Bible*. Philadelphia: Westminster Press, 1976.

Sennett, Richard. *Authority*. New York: Vintage Books, 1981.

Trible, Phyllis. *God and the Rhetoric of Sexuality*. Philadelphia: Fortress Press, 1978.

Walker, Alice. *The Color Purple*. New York: Harcourt Brace Jovanovich, 1982.

Weidman, Judith L. *Christian Feminism: Visions of a New Humanity*. New York: Harper & Row, 1984.

Wink, Walter. *Naming the Powers: The Language of Power in the New Testament*. Philadelphia: Fortress Press, 1984.